body language at work

Credits

Body Language at Work was conceived,
edited and designed by
Duncan Petersen Publishing Ltd,
31 Ceylon Road, London W14 OPY

The book is dedicated to the memory of Mel Petersen, Art Director and
co-founder of Duncan Petersen, who died in September 2001 while
working on this book. He courageously directed the photography for all the
main scenarios while suffering from a grave health problem.

Editorial Director: **Andrew Duncan**
In-house Art Director: **Mel Petersen**
Editor: **Chris Barstow**
Design Assistants: **Chris Foley** and
    Beverley Stewart
Outside Art Director: **Ben Cracknell**
Editorial Assistant: **Nicola Davies**
Photography: **Russell Sadur** and
    Peter Pugh-Cook

First published in Great Britain in 2003 by
Hamlyn, a division of Octopus Publishing Group Ltd
2–4 Heron Quays, London E14 4JP

Conceived, edited and designed by Duncan Petersen Limited
31 Ceylon Road
London W14 OPY

ISBN 0 600 60802 6

A CIP catalogue record for this book is available from the British Library

Printed and bound in China

10 9 8 7 6 5 4 3 2 1

hamlyn

body language at work

Read the Signs and Make the Right Moves

Hereford
SIXTH FORM COLLEGE
Learning Resources Centre

Peter Clayton

Contents

About the author

P eter Clayton is well known as a business development trainer, with 25 years' successful experience in sales and management.

He is the managing director of Sales Solutions & Training, which he founded in 1994 and provides specialist training consultancy to some of the UK's largest organizations. He regularly holds training courses and seminars in the UK, USA and Europe on selling, management, negotiation and presentation skills, but his passion lies with body language and behaviour profiling.

He first became interested in body language in 1982 and has spent the intervening years researching, studying, practising and teaching the subject.

In the last five years, his seminars and courses have highlighted the use of body language as an invaluable business tool. The ability to interpret the subtle and disguised gestures used in negotiation, selling, interviewing and people management can be the deciding factor between success or failure.

He is a motivational speaker who brings his expert advice and techniques into practical use for all sectors of industry and commerce, from induction level to senior management. He regularly works in the recruitment industry, training employment consultants to incorporate body language and profiling skills into the latest interviewing techniques.

He is a regular contributor to business trade journals and training newsletters and when he isn't lecturing or delivering seminars, he spends his time researching and writing new business development courses.

What is body language? I have asked countless people this question. Invariably the reply they give is something along the lines of 'non-verbal communication' – which I suppose is all right as far as it goes. However, it doesn't really illuminate the true nature of body language. Over the years, I have attempted to condense this into just a few simple sentences.

Try looking at it this way.

Normal conversation speed is around 100–120 words per minute. In the same amount of time, the average person can 'think' about 800 words. Body language is the outlet for this huge mass of unspoken thought and feeling.

Stop reading this book and study yourself for 24 hours, watching what happens to your body and voice when you feel happy, disappointed, angry, confused and so on. Notice the way your hands and arms, head and face all get excited when you are hearing something you enjoy. Conversely, notice how your body slows down when you are bored.

What is body language?

Why bother about it?

It is widely accepted that success in the world of work at the beginning of the 21st century is mainly achieved with or through other people. The days of the autocratic manager are long gone, and the average person today is far more confident and independent than in years gone by. If employees don't like the way they are being treated, they walk. A manager with bad body language will have them walking that much quicker.

If you've been around for a while, you will probably have discovered that good motivational and interpersonal skills – 'people skills', as they are known informally – are regarded as being just as important as paper qualifications were 30 years ago. Such skills cannot be mastered without an understanding of body language.

A necessary skill

Interpersonal skills used to be regarded as a bonus. Sales people had some rudimentary training in this field, but this was mainly concerned with handling objections – which by its very nature is adversarial. Managers were taught to

There's no harm in rehearsing your gestures in front of a mirror (left and right)

understand the importance of goal- and time-management, but little time was devoted to the way people reacted to being told what to do, or to being told off when they did not perform.

Even if you're a naturally good communicator – and, just as important, a good listener – your skills will never reach their full potential unless you understand body language. Research consistently shows that in any message, only half of the meaning is conveyed through the spoken word; the other half comes across in the speaker's body language.

Self-improvement

So if, like most of us, you're an average communicator, you are less likely to succeed if you have no awareness of body language. If you do, one of the greatest benefits is that it helps you to monitor your own performance, assess your own effectiveness, and improve on it.

I find it extraordinary that people skills such as body language aren't routinely taught at schools and colleges. For they *can* be taught – and taught quite easily, as I hope that this book will demonstrate.

Self-awareness and practice can help you achieve open, expressive body language (right)

In and out of work

I have centred this book around the types of body language that you will encounter in a wide range of day-to-day situations. Body language outside of the workplace is relatively easy to read; body language in a work environment tends to be much less obvious. Indeed, it is often disguised and deliberately played down, for the simple reason that at work, people often have to hide their true thoughts.

If you can understand the difficult body language of the workplace, you will have an excellent foundation for reading 'social' body language. Most of the principles are the same, and most of this book will serve you in and out of work. However, I have included a section devoted exclusively to special 'after hours' body language (see pages 114–133).

A starting point

It is useful to take a closer look at the differences between workplace and social behaviour, because it will give you an idea of the challenges involved in reading body language. Opposite are two sets of photographs, each showing two different individuals listening to a lecture. One set (above right) is of people in the back row; the other (below right) in the front.

Very bored

Uncertain and assessing the reaction of others

Back row

The body language of the back row is obvious, and easy to read without special knowledge. These individuals make no attempt to conceal whether they are bored, enthusiastic, disbelieving or whatever – in short, their reactions are unguarded. The reason is obvious: they are well hidden, over 30 metres (100 feet) away from the speaker. This kind of unmonitored body language is similar to what we all encounter outside the workplace.

Listening with rapt attention

Front row

The people in the front row are displaying the same range of feelings as those sitting at the back, but they are far better disguised, and reading their body language – without a trained eye – is much more of a challenge.

Critical and getting bored

Pitfalls

You might think that understanding body language is just a matter of common sense, but you'd be wrong: if spoken language is susceptible to misinterpretation, it's even truer of unspoken language. There are plenty of pitfalls when it comes to interpreting body language, and some of them can lead you badly astray.

Basic pitfall no. 1

The commonest mistake is trying to read body language in isolation, and making too hasty an assessment.

For example, there's a widespread belief that if someone scratches their nose, they must be lying; or that if someone's arms or legs are folded, it means they are fearful or anxious. It is far from being that simple, and this kind of amateur psychology can lead to a great deal of confusion. (For further examples of ambiguous body language, see Feet on the ground, page 28.)

Above all, don't try to learn individual signals. Instead, look at body language in terms of scenarios, just as we do in this book, where each piece of body language is described as it develops in specific situations, rarely in isolation.

Basic pitfall no. 2

Another common mistake is failing to monitor body language over a period of time. Recognizing the body language signal for, say, anger is one thing, but there is little point in doing so unless you can also determine the extent of that anger, and the course it is taking.

In the scenario opposite, Ted has been kept waiting for an appointment, and his anger level is rising with each passing minute. If you are the person who is keeping him waiting, you would do well to keep an eye on his body language, however busy you are – if you let the situation deteriorate too far, you can write off any positive outcome from your meeting.

Without feeling under pressure to react to every piece of body language you see, try at least to keep track of how many negative pieces of body language you're witnessing, and take action before too much damage is done.

One of the many benefits of studying body language is that it increases your self-awareness and your awareness of others. That, in turn, makes all of your encounters with other people more interesting and more rewarding.

2 pm Imagine you've scheduled an appointment with someone in their office. They keep you waiting in the reception area for five minutes. On a scale of ten, the level of anger you experience at this stage – if it registers at all – would probably rate as a one. If the door opened at that moment and someone came out, it wouldn't bother you if they didn't apologise.

At **2.10 pm** you are beginning to wonder what is happening. Your anger is up to level three.

At **2.20 pm** you are definitely expecting someone to come out and apologise for the delay. You're up to level five.

At **2.45 pm** you are still sitting unattended, and your anger level has risen to eight or nine; leaving the building seems to be the only way of reducing your blood pressure. To get you back down to level one or two would take a grovelling apology; without it, the meeting would have no chance of success.

This section explores a number of basic concepts – such as zones and personal territory – that you need to understand in order to appreciate fully the scenarios that make up the main part of the book.

It ends with particularly important advice on international variations in body language, which should be read together with the section on International etiquette (see pages 134–163).

The ability to read body language is closely related to the much-admired quality of emotional intelligence, which some people regard as being almost as important in the workplace as intellectual capacity. Unsurprisingly, women tend to score higher on emotional intelligence than men.

Body language basics

Territories and zones

Most of us know instinctively that we're territorial animals. It's not just that you feel irritated, or even slightly threatened, if another person comes in too close. You feel somehow invaded, even by apparently insignificant events such as someone opening their newspaper so that part of it intrudes on 'your' part of the table; or if it takes up empty space that you might want to occupy should you need to open *your* newspaper.

Bubbles

Anthropologists have written much on the subject. There seems to be little doubt that people's territorial responses are deep-rooted and primitive. Although some people manage to overcome them in part, they will never entirely go away. In business especially, you need to take them into account, precisely because when you're meeting people for the first time, you cannot know how just how irritated they will be by an accidental invasion of their social space.

Some experts make this topic very complicated, with many ifs and buts. I think that in the cut and thrust of work it needs to be straightforward and easy to remember. So I suggest that you simply imagine that everyone walks around in a bubble made of three invisible walls (see below and right).

Outer wall
The outer wall, around 2 metres (6 feet) in diameter, marks the outer limit of the 'business zone'. The space (shown here) between the outer wall and middle wall (see opposite) is where people can comfortably do business with you.

Middle wall

Between the middle wall and inner wall, at a distance of 30 centimetres–1.25 metres (2–4 feet), the 'personal zone' is for people you know and trust.

Inner wall

Within the inner wall, at a distance of between 30–60 centimetres (1–2ft) or closer, is the 'intimate zone'. For family and loved ones.

Territories and zones

At one point I worked with a sales representative who was very good at his job. I visited customers with him, and he got on well with them – or so I thought.

Once we were talking about the advantages of taking potential customers out for lunch or dinner. I took the commonplace view that it usually helped to build rapport – worth it for long-term customers. He surprised me by saying that he never found any good came of it.

Crowded

A while later, I found out why he was so sceptical. We took a customer out for a drink, and as we stood at the bar, my colleague came in so close to the customer that the customer began, very slowly, to inch away. In response, my colleague moved closer. After this had been repeated several times, the customer found an excuse to get right away from us: he went to make a phone call. When he came back, he made sure that I was sitting between him and my colleague, and addressed the rest of his conversation to me.

Dead end

Afterwards I couldn't decide whether to broach the subject with him – after all, he was great at his job. In the end, though, I did, asking him simply why it was that he stood so close to people. He said he had no idea that he had been doing it, or that it was a problem.

Town and country

Some experts believe that people who live in crowded environments need less social space than those who live in the country – so for example, a city-bred salesman selling to a farmer should remember to stand farther away than he would if his customer were a city-dweller. I'm not convinced that this is always good advice. It's true that city folk are used to having their social space invaded, but when it is, they are fairly quick to defend it with a stiffened, semi-aggressive posture that says, 'I've noticed that you've moved in closer; you can stay there, but be careful.' A country person might feel uncomfortable and unsure of how to deal with the invasion, but his response to it is likely to be less aggressive than that of his city cousin.

In this encounter between colleagues, A is playing by the rules: she's keeping just inside the personal zone – this is acceptable when there is trust between people who work together. But C has overstepped the invisible wall that should separate him from B.

A   B   C

B feels so uncomfortable with C that now she moves away and addresses A exclusively. A understands this, and tries to minimize the damage by carefully staying on the edge of the personal zone. If you find yourself in C's position, ask yourself whether you have invaded someone's zone.

B   A   C

Clusters

This sounds like an impressive piece of jargon – but it's no big deal. It simply means several pieces of body language happening at the same time, or one after another over a short period. You could liken a single piece of body language to a sentence: it makes a single statement.

A cluster, then, is like several sentences together – in other words, a paragraph. In the main part of this book most of the illustrations are of clusters.

Below is an 'anxiety cluster' which occurs as Sarah is trying to understand what a speaker is saying.

1 Puzzled, anxious

2 Still puzzled – so even more anxious

3 Anxiously trying to focus again

4 Still can't understand – sags with defeat

Congruence

This is another impressive-sounding term for something quite simple.

Congruence occurs when thoughts and words are in tune with one another, and are corroborated by the body. It is what you, see for example, when a speaker is being sincere. It doesn't necessarily mean that he or she is being 100 per cent honest; but it does mean that someone believes in what they are saying or the spirit in which they are saying it.

Congruent body language must be read as part of a cluster (see pages 22, and 24–25). If it is followed by a series of congruent gestures, then the chances are you can put your faith in what you have just heard. Subsequent conflicting body language should make you question what is being said, and seek further reassurance.

Example: Ted has just won a huge contract for his recruitment agency to supply 50 local construction workers to a national property development company, with the opportunity to repeat the process in other major towns.

His boss congratulates him in front of his co-workers, shaking his hand and telling him what a great job he has done. Ted's head is tilted upwards and he is smiling with the upper and lower half of his face. He turns and makes eye contact with his colleagues, gesturing towards all of them with open palm as he tells his boss that he couldn't have done it without their support. Not everyone had helped, in fact a couple were going to do some research for him, but let him down. Right now, however, in his euphoria, Ted includes everyone.

Non-congruence

Non-congruent body language, where the gestures contradict the words, is a sign of inner turmoil and should not be trusted. You have to work out what the problem might be: it doesn't have to be a blatant lie – it could simply be a sign that a speaker is paying lip service, does not wish to offend or is just uncomfortable.

Again, non-congruent body language must be read in clusters.

Bear in mind that non congruent body language betrays not just conflict between what a speaker is sayng and thinking, but what they in turn are hearing from you or others present.

Clusters

Sometimes it is easy to mistake a body language cluster for something it isn't, such as relaxed posture, or indeed neutral body language.

The sequence shown below is a case in point. John looks, on the face of it, as if he is cautiously interested by what he is hearing. The reality is somewhat different.

1 Perhaps the most interesting thing about a cluster is that it can indicate either a change of mood or that a particular state of mind has been reached. Here, John looks cautiously interested, but he is leaning back with his head tilted up, and his forefingers are pointing downwards – negative signs.

2 The negative signs we have just observed are now confirmed by John quickly folding his arms to make a kind of defensive barrier. At the same time, there's an undeniable look of surprise on his face. However, he's still trying to appear interested in order not to offend the colleague who is speaking.

Masquerading

Sadly, there are plenty of people around who want to look like the boss: perhaps they imagine that this may favour them over someone less assertive when it comes to promotion.

This kind of posturing – masquerading – is easy to spot if you are sensitive to clusters. Too many gestures, or too many short, quick movements, repeated in groups, at intervals, are give-away signs. 'Standing tall', or 'towering', is another give-away. Is this person relaxed in their upright posture, or too stiff? Peppering speech with business terms is yet another tell-tale sign, perhaps in combination with the above. If you keep hearing senior management jargon such as 'bottom line' or 'risk-to-reward ratio', you may well be listening to a 'wannabee' rather than the real thing.

3 A big change has taken place. John is now interested in what is being said and displays the body language of someone who is listening with full attention. He's leaning forwards, trunk square-on to the speaker, and although he may or may not agree with what's being said, he's committed.

International variations

This book is essentially about body language you will encounter at work in the western world – western Europe, the USA and Canada. Most of the body language I discuss in the main part of the book crosses most of the frontiers in these parts of the world, and much of it can travel to other parts of the world without causing misunderstandings or uneasy feelings.

However, a few aspects of 'Western' body language *can* get you into trouble when you travel abroad. They are discussed on these two pages.

Global etiquette

If you're doing business internationally, you need to be aware of specific local customs concerning etiquette, casual greetings and so on. For example, the Japanese usually present their business cards while holding them in both hands; Indians greet not with a handshake but with palms held together in a prayer gesture – the *namaste*. If Westerners don't reciprocate, they rarely cause offence; if they do reciprocate, it can help to oil the wheels. (For extensive coverage of such customs, see international etiquette, pages 134–163.)

Crunch points

Pitfall: Eye contact
Who should take note?
Any westerner visiting the Far East, particularly Japan and Korea.
Damage limitation
The Japanese and other Asians find too much direct eye contact aggressive and rude. So, tone down your eye contact.

Pitfall: Business cards
Who should take note?
Any westerner visiting Japan.
Damage limitation
To the Japanese, visiting cards are not just bits of stiff card with names printed on them: they are part of their owner's identity, and accordingly are treated with great respect. When you first receive a card, take time to study it; then put it carefully on the table in front of you. When the meeting is finished, put it in your wallet, not in a pocket, and especially not in a hip pocket – that means you could sit on it. Those Japanese who frequently travel abroad are of course becoming aware of the western approach to business cards, but for the many with no foreign experience, this is still quite a sensitive point.

Pitfall: Waving goodbye
Who should take note?
North Americans visiting Mediterranean Europe and Latin America.
Damage limitation
The normal American gesture for waving goodbye can be taken as 'No' in these parts of the world. It's best to avoid the gesture.

Pitfall: Touching other people
Who should take note?
Everyone, wherever they go.
Damage limitation
Touching someone on the arm to make a point as you speak, putting a hand on their shoulder, or even on their hand, all come very naturally to some cultures. These innocent gestures are often tokens of trust or approval, useful reinforcers of confidence, and helpful in emphasizing points while communicating. But they can also offend or even annoy, depending on who you are dealing with. In general, nationalities divide into three groups (right) when it comes to touching.

Tactility

1 Not very tactile
In Japan, the United States and Canada, the UK, Scandinavia and other Northern European countries, also in Australia and Estonia, touching is generally kept to a minimum, with some important exceptions. Avoid heartily slapping a Japanese on the back, or putting an arm round his shoulders in a gesture of friendship or congratulation – he'll feel very uncomfortable.

2 Somewhat tactile
In France, China, Ireland and India, touching is somewhat more acceptable.

3 Tactile
In Middle Eastern countries, Latin America, Italy, Greece, Spain, Portugal, some Asian countries and Russia, touching is common, and much more acceptable. In fact, some Arabian businessmen may actually take your hand as you walk along as a gesture of special respect and rapport.

Feet on the ground

Before progressing to the next section of this book, don't forget that many of the body language indicators that you read about here can, on occasion, have an all-too-mundane – rather than a psychological – meaning. In other words, always keep your feet on the ground, and don't try to read any one piece of body language in isolation: sometimes, an itch is just an itch.

Scratching the nose

Hands in pockets

Folded arms

Body language	Could mean	Often means
Scratching the nose	Lying, disbelief	Itchy nose
Leaning back in chair	Superiority, arrogance	Feels relaxed; tired
Hands in pockets	Secretive, withdrawn, perhaps depressed	Hands feel cold; feeling for coin
Folded arms	Defensive, uncertain, in need of reassurance	It's cold; feels comfortable
Crossed legs	Defensive, repressed, possibly hostile	It's comfortable (men); it's feminine (women)
Yawning	Difficult situation; bored	Tired; poor air supply

Crossed legs
(men)

Crossed legs
(women)

Yawning

Leaning back in chair

You don't have authority over your boss, and you probably can't give orders to your husband, wife or difficult colleagues, either. Most days of your life, though, situations arise in which you want to persuade these people to change their minds. You can't tell them, so you have to sell to them.

'Sell' is not a dirty word: most sales people are decent men and women who want to provide a service. The right body language can help you to communicate this message about yourself when you sell – which is why this section starts by looking at how to achieve trust and create good first impressions through the handshake.

It then looks at body language in two standard sales situations – around a table, and selling to a small group.

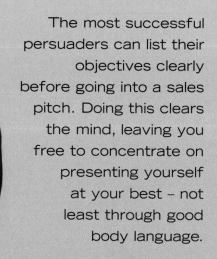

The most successful persuaders can list their objectives clearly before going into a sales pitch. Doing this clears the mind, leaving you free to concentrate on presenting yourself at your best – not least through good body language.

Selling and persuading

Achieving trust

Before you can get anywhere as a sales person – in fact before you can persuade anyone to do anything – you have to achieve a measure of trust.

Some people expect to be trusted in three minutes, but this invariably slows things down. Most of us forget how personal a matter trust is, and forget to make proper allowance for the different speeds at which different personality types are capable of moving towards trust.

As we will see in the following pages, using the right body language is the key to achieving trust. But there are several other important factors to bear in mind:

Trust is achieved incrementally

In business, just as in personal life, you can only build trust one step at a time. You can have it one minute, and lose it the next. If you think you're doing well, trust your instinct and carry on to finish the job, but expect to repeat the process. Newcomers to sales often think they've finished the job at the first meeting, and then behave as if they're trusted. In reality, they're seen as pushy, and often lose any trust they did manage to gain at an earlier stage.

Watch the zones

Standing close irritates, and may even intimidate. Remember, the business zone starts at about 1.25 metres (4 feet) from your customer.

Get the handshake right

See page 36.

Get their name right

Dale Carnegie, father of self-improvement authors, summed it up when he said that the sweetest sound in anyone's ears is the sound of their own name. But don't overdo it, like third-rate sales people do: repeating someone's name at regular intervals is annoying, insincere and over-familiar.

Don't talk too much

Avoid gabbling: it makes you sound shallow, and suggests a lack of interest in anything your customer might have to say.

Smile with your eyes

It's important to smile, but it's equally important not to overdo it.

Smiling indicates that you are a friendly, open, approachable person, and hints that you are likely to be a fair negotiator. If you remain tight-lipped, you will send the message that you are either nervous or unreceptive – neither of which will help you sell.

If, on the other hand, you enter the room beaming broadly your customer they may wonder what you have to be so pleased about so early in the transaction.

When you first meet, smile with the eyes rather than the whole face. This is a useful precaution because it's easy for someone to tell if you are trying too hard to smile. At a later stage, you can try out whole-face smiles and watch for the customer's reaction.

If you just don't feel in the mood, it's time to use your acting skills: relax your facial muscles and recall a pleasurable experience, or a good friend. With practice, this will bring the easy, encouraging smile that helps engender relaxed, open negotiating situations.

Achieving trust

Delivery

Mirror as much as you can of your customer's speech – pitch, tone, resonance and volume. These can all be highly expressive of how someone is thinking at any given moment. People like people who think the way they do.

The way you talk: speed

You can think many times faster than you can talk, and because of that it's natural to start talking before someone else has finished. You know how bad it can feel when someone does it to you – so make a resolution now never to do it again to someone you want to persuade or sell to.

Hands

As will be seen throughout this book, people tend to use their hands spontaneously to emphasize what they're saying or to signal that it is sincere. When they're exaggerating, concealing or lying, hand movements are generally reduced; sometimes hands are placed out of the way, in pockets or behind a desk. To establish trust, let your hand movements be seen, and let them flow naturally.

Eye contact

Unless you're dealing with a dominant or difficult type, keep your gaze generally into the lower part of the face, below the eyes. This is sometimes known as the 'intimate' gaze, but it is better described as the

Crossing arms and legs

Avoid crossing your arms and legs when selling – especially to a new customer. It can look casual, whether you mean to be or not. If, however, your customer takes the lead by crossing arms or legs, then it can be useful to 'mirror' him or her.

Mirroring

Mirroring (above) can be a very potent body language; it communicates liking and respect for the person you are dealing with. Follow their gestures with similar ones of your own a few seconds later – but take care not to be too obvious about it.

'generally acceptable' gaze. Don't go for too much eyeball-to-eyeball gazing – continuous eye contact (see page 110) may be taken as a sign of insincerity, even lying.

If you need to underline an important point by making eye contact, I recommend staring at the cheek bones instead. It's perfectly friendly, and less intimidating than full eye contact.

Be careful, however, that you don't give the impression of deliberately avoiding eye contact; this can suggest that you are being evasive, that you lack confidence, or that you are simply not interested in the matter at hand.

Handshakes

There are those who would prefer to do away with handshaking on the grounds that it's an empty ritual, but human interactions are full of ritual and, like it or not, handshakes are often the first piece of body language that you will experience in any business encounter.

Conventional wisdom has it that you can learn volumes about a person from their handshake, but I'm sceptical of this, as you'll see over the following pages. I've tried to confine this book's coverage of the topic to the few basic facts of which we can be reasonably certain.

On the most basic level, a poor handshake can certainly create confusion – even mirth – and it's probably true to say that if you get your own handshake right, it will help you to make a positive first impression, thereby laying the groundwork for trust.

Types of handshake

I have chosen not to complicate this subject by introducing too many subtle variations on the basic shake. Instead, we look at mainstream handshakes for everyday scenarios.

The significance of handshakes

In primitive societies the hand held forward to be shaken – or possibly up in the air, wide open for all to see – may have been a sign that you came unarmed and in peace. It's a nice theory, but don't let it colour your judgement of people on first meeting. There are too many ifs and buts about handshaking for it to be a reliable guide to character.

Take, for example, the British. They are generally much less keen on shaking hands than their mainland European neighbours, who are capable of beginning and ending the shortest business encounter with a comradely shake, even if they know the person well. For the British, handshaking is a more formal procedure, and it tends to be confined to meetings between people who are not on familiar terms. (For other important cultural differences when meeting, greeting and generally getting along with people of different nationalities, see International etiquette, pages 134–163.)

The 'keep your distance' handshake

This is the classic, ceremonial handshake, appropriate when you are meeting someone for the first time. (The descriptions in this section all refer to the person on the right). Keep your shaking arm outstretched but not too high, your posture upright. The hand is held horizontally, with the palm facing to the left. The clasp should be of medium pressure – too firm, and you'll appear over-assertive; not firm enough, and you'll come across as passive. Take the other person's hand fully – at the palm, not by the fingers. Done in this way, the shake sends a reasonable message: 'We are meeting on equal terms. I don't want to be unfriendly, but before we get down to business, there's more I want to know about you.' It can be a good idea to hold on to the person's hand for a moment longer than you would do naturally – literally holding his or her attention while the opening pleasantries are exchanged.

Handshakes

The 'dominant' shake

The palm-down handshake is said to come naturally to dominant or difficult types (see page 88), but don't fall into the trap of believing that this is always the case. There are plenty of weak characters around who have been told that use of the 'dominant' handshake is an effective way of assuming dominance in a relationship.

Sometimes, these types give themselves away by extending the arm with palm already face down, before even making contact. However, much as they might wish they were born leaders, people who execute this sort of manoeuvre usually are not – they just need help.

Far more characteristic of the genuinely dominant shake is to begin in the usual, palms-facing mode – perhaps with the palm slightly bent over – then, during the shake, to turn the other person's hand firmly into a palm-up, or nearly palm-up, position. Of course, this movement must be deft, or it could just seem clumsy – so you should use it only if you are confident that you can pull it off. People who do it effectively can take you by surprise, sending the message, 'I'm going to be in charge here' – or, to put it another way, 'I've got the upper hand'.

Dominant hand on right

'You're trusted'

Similar to the 'you're welcome in my space' shake, but now the proximity is even closer (left). The handshake lasts longer, and the hands travel farther up and down . It's used instinctively by those on friendly terms, or by trusted associates. If someone uses this shake the first time they meet you, it can indicate that they are very confident of their ability, but it can also be a sign of over-familiarity, so use it with caution.

'You're welcome in my space'

Similar to the 'keep your distance' shake (see page 37), but here (right) the parties are several inches closer to each other, signalling a friendlier approach. The arm is bent at the elbow, and the hand may be bent at the wrist to keep it parallel to the ground – although this can create an impression of assumed superiority. (To avoid this, let your hand slant upwards.) It's a subtler, more collaborative way of influencing a relationship than the dominant shake (opposite), and requires a lesser degree of self-projection, not to mention self-assurance.

Handshakes

'Real pals'

Similar to 'you're trusted' (see page 39), but you move in even closer. Reserved for friends and closest associates. Don't use this on strangers to impress them with your friendliness. The shake (below) involves entering their personal zone (see page 18), and many will take this – consciously or subconsciously – as threatening, or, at the least, irritating.

Grasping someone else's forearm or shoulder with your free hand as you shake (below) will almost certainly make them think that you are both cocksure and insincere. The same goes for the truly nauseating 'politician's handshake' (bottom), where both hands are clasped over the other person's – usually as the perpetrator leans forward and fixes his victim with a concerned gaze. When polls are taken on the subject, politicians consistently rank among the least trusted people in society. They could fool us more effectively if they paid greater attention to their body language.

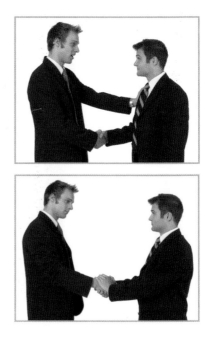

Good handshakes ...

A good handshake feels comfortable – neither too firm nor too limp. It doesn't feel clammy, either: if you sweat easily, make sure that your palm is dry by (discreetly) wiping it before you shake.

... the bad and the ugly handshake

The over-firm shake (illustrated in an admittedly extreme form below) is supposed to imply confidence, but many will think it's aggressive, and may want to keep you at a distance once they know you use it – or they may think it's done deliberately, to give the impression of a dominance you don't actually possess.

By contrast, the weak handshake is meant to imply low self-confidence. Avoid this kind of shake, but don't read too much into it if you're on the receiving end. I have met many people who are as unbending as a reinforced steel joist, but are still full-time purveyors of the limpest handshakes.

Seating plans for sales

Read these two pages in conjunction with the section on negotiating (pages 60–75). Much of the advice applies to both, particularly the importance of identifying the main decision-maker, and of taking along someone who can observe the other side's body language while your mind is on delivering the sales presentation.

Table talk

Good seating plans help to create good body language. For example, avoid the seating plan shown above and in the diagram, right, unless you are selling from a position of strength – when you know the other side needs the business more than you do; or if you are making a very formal presentation.

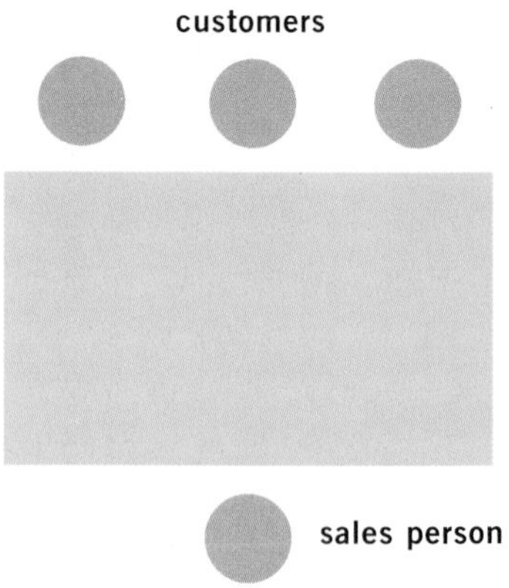

customers

sales person

The centre line

Human beings, even laid-back types, can't help being territorial animals. If you sit opposite anyone at a table, there's always an invisible centre line that marks in the minds of everyone present the boundary of their side of the table. If your briefcase, a presentation portfolio or even a single sheet of paper strays across the line, you are, in effect, invading their space. It seems absurd that this should cause resentment, but it always does, to some extent.

Minimizing confrontation

It's no coincidence that round tables are used often in offices – they not only encourage co-operative body language, but are efficient space fillers. If you are a sales person and want your customer to feel that little bit better, let him or her sit with their back to a wall.

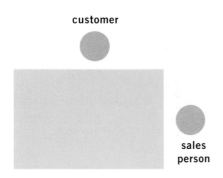

customer

sales
person

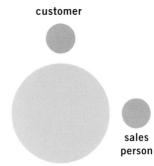

customer

sales
person

The arrangement above is not just for sales pitches. It is useful for most one-to-one meetings, especially where a senior person wants informality and rapport with a junior: glancing down regularly at paperwork, then to one side to catch the junior's eye with a friendly glance is a good way to do this.

If you can, sit at 45 degrees to your customer, as above. This avoids territorial confrontation and uses the corner of the desk as a partial barrier. The customer feels unthreatened, and the sales person can get useful half-on eye contact, which is not as challenging as face-on eye contact.

Seating plans for sales

The briefcase manoeuvre

If you go into a sales pitch where the seating obliges you to sit opposite the customers, use the technique illustrated below to work your way round to the end of the table so you can present from the corner position. The added advantage of this manoeuvre is that it creates a degree of informality. The customer sees a sales person who is busy rather than static, not a bad thing, provided it's done in a smooth sequence. The moves have to be timed carefully to fill in interludes in the sales discussion – which there will of course be, since customers should never be bombarded with continuous talk.

sales person

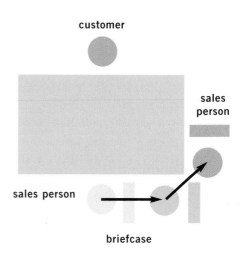

customer

sales person

sales person

briefcase

1 Sit down on the chair, putting your briefcase on the floor to your right; place it so that it is marginally out of reach, making sure that you look relaxed and natural as you do this.

2 Pretend that you've forgotten to take something out of it, and move your chair a little closer in order to reach it. Take out your papers, then put the briefcase down on the floor again – this time, a little farther to the right.

3 Repeat this process until you are sitting where you want to be, at the end of the table, diagonally opposite the customer. Now you can make your presentation from a more relaxed, less confrontational position.

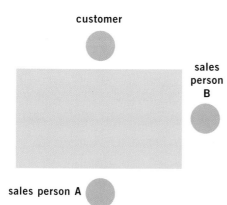

customer

sales person B

sales person A

Team work

The seating plan shown above can work well if two sales people are visiting a single customer. The one sitting opposite (sales person A) should be the one who will actually operate the account, and will have had a previous meeting with the customer.

The one sitting in the corner position (sales person B) should be a colleague of sales person A, who has had prior experience of the customer's business.

Sales person B engages the customer by asking him to reminisce about his previous experiences with outside suppliers, and empathizes with any problems he may have had. Now he turns to sales person A, and asks him how he would overcome these problems, inviting the customer to join in. Sales person B and the customer end up playing a duet. The customer starts to feel that sales person B is almost a customer too, and that sales person A is, in a sense, their 'adversary'.

Musical chairs

If several sales people and customers are present, try to engineer an alternating seating arrangement, to avoid an 'us and them' situation.

Highly formal presentations are an exception to this rule – a mixed seating plan would be considered unprofessional in this context. The tried and tested approach – the sales person standing at one end of the table with a flip chart or other sales materials – is probably the most effective.

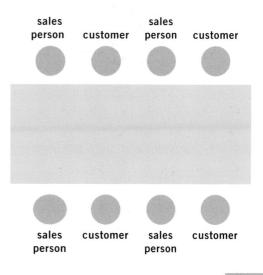

sales person customer sales person customer

sales person customer sales person customer

Selling to small groups

Selling alone to a small group is difficult – it's virtually impossible to sell well and at the same time be fully tuned to the other side's body language. For that reason, this scenario deliberately concentrates on the single most important thing to keep in mind during your pitch: *include all of your customers.* You must be continually on the look-out for body language that tells you one or other of your customers is losing interest.

As you start talking, tell yourself to sell to everyone. Keep your body language animated, and the hands up (see page 52). At the same time, ask yourself who among your customers is the key decision-maker – just as you should when negotiating (see pages 72–73).

When you have identified that person, don't make the mistake of selling to him or her exclusively: the decision-maker sometimes prefers a passive role, leaving the talking to others, and wants to be left alone to think. But be alert for the following sequence of body language which not only identifies the decision-maker, but tells you whether he or she is reacting positively or negatively.

1 Honeymoon period

In a formal presentation (see left), the customers will usually start with their bodies close to the table, in a relatively upright posture – interested in what the seller has to say, and ready to give him or her a chance. Make the most of this 'honeymoon' period, and go in with your strongest shot – if you build slowly, you may have lost your customers' attention before you deliver your killer point. Incidentally, the sales pitch would go much better with the horseshoe seating arrangement shown on page 59.

2 Dropping away

Be on the alert for the slightest movement away from the table: in the scenario above, Ted, seated centre, may still look interested, but a space of even a couple of inches between him and the edge of the table is a potential danger sign. Here, he has dropped well away from the table. However, there's no need to panic: he could simply be analyzing the situation, and the extent of his disinterest (or displeasure) will depend on many other subtle signs (see pages 73 and 75).

Selling to small groups

3 Cloning the boss

In the scenario above, the two colleagues on either side of Ted are doing exactly the same thing: they are 'mirroring' their boss's body language, which is something subordinates tend to do automatically. Each may well turn slightly towards Ted, too.

The body language in our scenario should confirm to the seller that Ted is the sole decision-maker. It should also indicate

that the pitch has not gone well – Ted and his colleagues are leaning back in their chairs, away from the negotiating space, arms folded defensively – and that unless the seller now says something to recapture his attention, it could fail altogether. It's difficult to advise how best to move things forward in such a delicate situation, but a retrieval strategy is proposed on the opposite page.

4 Retrieval tactics

When you sense that a sale is slipping away from you, it's generally best to carry on rather than stop to find out what's wrong. Talk on until you reach the next natural stopping-place, then say, 'I've plenty more to say, but perhaps you'd like to give me your reactions before I go any further.' You then listen to the objections, note them down, and ask if you can return to them later, after you've finished making your presentation. A more experienced seller might carry on talking, but change tack to see if he can bring Ted back on side. To do this, you need to be able to put yourself in your customer's shoes, identify the areas where you might be failing to respond to his needs, then propose solutions.

This short section is primarily for those whose work involves talking (which includes selling) to groups of typically 7–10 people, but occasionally more. It is also aimed at anyone who has to stand up and face an audience from time to time. It'll be useful, too, if you have to give a speech at a dinner.

These pages also complement pages 46–49 where I look at body language for those who have to sell to small groups. You should read them together, if possible: the comparisons are quite interesting.

Even perfect body language technique (if it were possible) won't help you to speak better in public if you suffer badly from nerves. There's no easy way to overcome a dry mouth and a beating heart, but you can help yourself by thorough preparation: read your notes so often that you almost know them by heart. Also, just before speaking, try to find a moment – if possible with the eyes closed – to clear your mind by visualizing a pleasant, calming scene, such as a lake at sunset, with ducks diving and fish languidly rising.

Presentations, lectures and addresses

The presenter

As you might have guessed, the demands are merciless. You've got to keep your body language up to standard all the time. Obviously, addressing an audience is different from talking to one person. On these two pages are some basic tips on good and bad self-presentation when standing to address an audience.

Joan

Good
Head up, arms out, appealing to the audience to listen – you are assuming control and everything begins when you do. The whole body is on view, and you must establish a whole-body approach from the start.

Good
Some arm movement to emphasize your opening remarks conveys confidence in what you're saying, and a lively approach. Before a word is said, a strong image has been projected.

Not bad

More positive body language: the front of the body is still fully exposed to the audience, which sends a confident message even though Joan is pointing to the flip chart.

Bad

Standing still and talking in a normal conversational voice sends the message 'I'm nervous'. Hands in pockets denote lack of enthusiasm.

The presenter

Going downhill ...

Rocker

Realizing she should be a little more active, Joan starts rocking forwards and backwards on the same spot. Once started, this is hard to stop. For the audience, it's tortuous. At its worst, it can look deranged. To escape this common trap, she needs to start moving around and using her voice to animate the important points.

Figleaf

Now Joan is really struggling to keep control. You'll often see this bad body language – known as a figleaf gesture – following soon after the rocking motion described left. In this context you'd be right to interpret the 'figleaf' as a throw-back to the jungle, when submissive and nervous primates made genital-shielding gestures in order to calm themselves before a dominating presence. Hands behind the back is a similar type of mistake, conveying lack of confidence. It's much better to let your hands dangle loosely by your sides and move them occasionally to emphasize points.

Worse and worse ...

Reading the lesson

Here Joan has started reading from her notes. It looks as if she has no idea what to say next. The lectern should effectively be invisible, or, at best, a prop you don't really need. Here it looks as if the lectern is in charge. The best way to avoid this disastrous scenario is to learn your lines by heart, so that knowing what to say next does not become an issue. This frees you up to concentrate on maximum performance.

Crash

In this picture she tries a more relaxed pose by leaning on the lectern, but rather than being relaxed and in control, she looks too casual, perhaps even sloppy. And what if the lectern can't take her weight?

The presenter

Now Joan really goes head first towards disaster – but just about manages to salvage it at the end. As well as correcting her body language, she needs to vary her tone of voice, trying to make it as rich as possible.

If you have to use an overhead projector, place the material for projection quickly and squarely on the projector. Audiences tire all too easily if the change-overs are slow and messy.

Disaster
Getting little reaction from the audience, Joan has started to stare at the screen for inspiration. Her voice has lost its sparkle and sounds as if she is reading a speech.

Lost it
This sequence of hand-to-ear and hand-to-face gestures suggest that Joan is concealing the fact that she's struggling to think straight, and that she has doubts about what she's saying. Speakers who are in trouble often do them together in a sequence.

Resurrection

Joan now has one chance of pulling back from the brink of the worst presentation of her life. She should scan the audience for anyone who nods their heads on making eye contact with her. However badly the speaker is doing, there's usually a dedicated handful who agree with what she's saying, find it interesting and want her to succeed – in fact they'd be riveted if her body language wasn't so awful. Joan should now deliver her presentation to them, forgetting the rest of audience. If they respond – and often they do – this will be the magic ingredient to get her back on track for the whole group.

The audience

Even a first-class presentation can go wrong if the seating is unsympathetic to listener and speaker. A common mistake is to have the speaker too close to the audience: strangers are embarrassed and ill at ease if their space is invaded (see page 18).

Addressing dinners

The advice on these pages holds good for after-dinner speakers, except of course you probably don't have to worry about proximity to those seated next to you – you'll be on easy terms and there will be no problem about invading territory. Nevertheless, it can be more of a challenge to face a small audience than a larger one, as the address will resemble a conversation more than a lecture.

You should address your listeners individually, as if they are participants rather than a passive herd. Maintain a second or two of eye contact with each person, plus five seconds or so of addressing each one in turn, but without staring. You will need to be extra aware of timing; allow for listeners' silent responses to your points.

Bistro-style seating

Round tables with about six people per table at each make the listeners far more relaxed than straight rows and this often communicates positively to the speaker.

However, this arrangement can make the listeners territorial. They may join together as teams and challenge – or champion – the speaker, and they may get competitive with the people at the other table.

Horseshoe seating

It's no coincidence that the 'horseshoe' is so often preferred for small- to medium-sized presentations. The speaker can enter the central area in order to achieve closer rapport with the listeners, but without invading their social space – they are safely the other side of the table.

However, the presenter must make continual use of the lighthouse technique for addressing the group (below), or some listeners will feel left out. This seating arrangement often means that the presenter gets plenty of questions, even debate, because the audience can all see each other and so they all feel involved.

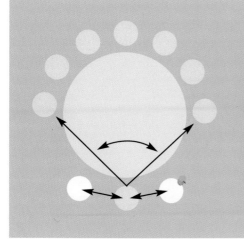

Lighthouse technique

This is fundamental: swivel your body from right to left, and back again, briefly making eye contact with as many members of the audience as possible – preferably each member. Move position as you do this.

At the best of times, it's hard to concentrate on business tactics at the same time as closely observing your opposite number's body language. In this section, we deal with the most testing occasions of all: when the preliminaries are over and there's a deal that has to be closed, or a conflict that must be resolved, often against the clock.

It's not surprising that supremely successful operators try under these conditions to gain every small advantage. I'm not suggesting that you wear dark glasses to prevent your opposite number seeing into your eyes – there's a much simpler option, increasingly followed as a matter of course by go-ahead businesses. Take someone with you as a body language observer.

The scenario described on pages 72–75 is based on a real-life situation where I was present as a body language observer.

Many aspects of life
– even personal life – involve
negotiation. Before you go into
a negotiation you should have a
clear understanding of what it
is that you want to achieve,
and how far you are prepared
to compromise. If your
knowledge of body language
can gain you an insight into
your opponent's strategy, so
much the better.

Negotiating

A negotiator's basics

There are few places as delicate and tense as the negotiating table, and it could be said that this is where body language awareness is at its most essential. Eyes and (especially) hands may tell you more of what you need to know about your opponents than words, and entire businesses and livelihoods may depend on how you interpret the signs.

And, of course, it's not just judging your opponents – your own body language may betray far more than you realize. If you look too relaxed it will seem as if you lack a professional approach, or,

Not what I want
Clenching the hands means either frustration or a negative attitude towards an offer that has just been made.

I know my game
Composed, direct gaze, hands resting calmly in lap, head slightly to one side in mild challenge: all suggest supreme confidence. If he now steeples his hands, the message will be even stronger.

alternatively, that you are trying too hard to bluff about how in control you are. It's easy to slip into bad body language, so be aware of the signs. An alert posture will maximize your concentration – sit up straight, let your shoulders relax and keep hands out of sight and away from possible distractions such as pens. If you are negotiating over the phone, the same guidelines apply, as things like bad posture or inattentiveness are detectable in the voice, especially by another experienced negotiator. You may find it's better to stand.

Meeting's as good as over

It would be a waste of time trying to convince this negotiator of anything. He's so relaxed with his position that he's loosened his posture to the brink of informality and he looks at you with faint pity in his eyes. Arms folded, thumbs visible, pointing up, send the same message.

Mustn't lose it

Rubbing the back of the neck suggests that someone is trying to control negative feelings about an offer made or position reached.

A negotiator's basics

Looking at these two pages, and the previous two, please bear in mind my warning about placing too much faith in body language seen in isolation (see page 14).

Visualizing

This negotiator is experiencing action replay. His move back and forth, 'seeing' what happened.

Better take it seriously

If he's slowly stroking his chin it suggests your ideas are being carefully considered.

Wasting my time

If he rests his head on one thumb, which is hidden by his hand, it suggests that you are being boring and that the negotiation could be going downhill fast.

What?!

If the person you are negotiating with blinks several times in succession, it usually denotes shock or that he didn't want to hear what you just said.

On my own now

Closing his eyes for a few seconds with his head down, and his breathing noticeable, reveals his fear about the decision being made. This could well be followed by ...

... I need space to think

If he looks up, perhaps with a smile, he may be remembering some inspiration that's got him out of trouble in the past. This could mean any decision will be postponed.

A negotiating predicament

John and Chris have a meeting to negotiate the final price of a major new contract. John knows a little about body language and adopts some challenging postures in order to try to gain an edge: he leans back confidently in his chair, arms hidden behind his back, suggesting that he's not in a mood to be open. He avoids being drawn into small talk about the holiday he's just taken.

Chris is not nearly so confident, uncertain of how to play it because he hasn't been able to talk to his boss before the meeting about how low a price he can accept from this important new customer.

John

Chris

1 Tough

John intensifies his advantage by looking at his notes while he speaks, avoiding eye contact with Chris. He coolly announces that Chris is going to be disappointed with the price, and names a very low figure.

2 Appraisal

John sneaks a quick look at Chris to gauge his response. Chris's hand rests lightly on his cheek, forefinger pointing upwards. John recognizes this as a sign that the offer is being analyzed – but not necessarily with favour. John concludes that Chris needs the business badly enough not to reject it outright – a fair guess, but one which doesn't turn out to be right.

A negotiating predicament

3 Stall

Chris now says that he believes John can do better, but as he does so, John notices Chris's sequence of hand-to-face and hand-to-neck gestures, indicating discomfort and uncertainty. John now restates his offer in a very controlled, flat voice – a real killer in such situations. It sends the unspoken message that John is completely unmoved by what Chris has to say. He reinforces this dominant approach with a steady gaze at the forehead (see page 91), and by blinking less frequently, which intensifies the 'fearless' directness of his gaze (below).

Chris now feels so uncomfortable that he decides to stall. He suggests that they break for 15 minutes while he phones his office to check out whether he can move down towards Bob's price by getting cheap bulk delivery.

4 Bluff called

Chris is back from the phone. His boss has told him that he'd rather lose the business than go as low as Bob's price. As a result, Chris has some of his confidence back – if only because he knows where he stands.

This is reflected unconsciously in his body language: he doesn't feel exactly good, but his frame is now held relatively still and solid; his voice is controlled and he doesn't bother with eye contact, as he quietly says, 'Sorry, this is not going to work.'

A negotiating predicament

5 Outmanoeuvered

John's eyes close, his head goes down, and he gives a low sigh, all obvious signs of exasperation, not lost on Chris, who now coolly insists that if John wants the goods, he'll have to come up with a much larger order in order to achieve a realistic price.

6 John's response

As John admits that he might be able to reconsider, his tight, closed body language is obvious. In another context, the interlocked fingers could mean obstinate refusal to listen, but here they mean much the same as arms folded defensively across the torso. John's shoulders are slightly hunched up, too, another sign that he is on the back foot.

7 Back in the game

Much to John's irritation, he now notices
Chris's hands being quickly rubbed together,
suggesting a pleasurable sense of
satisfaction or expectation. Chris is clearly
relieved to be back in the game. Slow
rubbing or wringing the hands, by the way,
would suggest that Chris thinks he's
successfully taking advantage – not the
case in this instance.

Group negotiations

Big, complex deals are often negotiated by teams with several members, each responsible for one aspect of the deal – financial, technical, and so on. Increasingly, go-ahead organizations send along a body language specialist too.

The essence of his or her job is to identify who, on the opposite side, is the overall decision-maker. That person's reactions can be subtle and difficult to spot, but they are often the key to how things are really going, rarely obvious because experienced negotiators try to hide their true feelings, giving the impression that things are more difficult than they expected.

Ted

John

1 Magnastruct v Baker Chemicals

Magnastruct's team has several members, including its body language expert, Ted. Magnastruct is a construction company selected to build a new lab for Baker Chemicals – provided terms can be agreed.

Baker Chemicals' team likewise has several members, but the only one who is relevant to this story is John, not only a major shareholder, but the finance director, and ultimately the man who makes the decisions. Ted will be keeping a close eye on him.

2 Half an hour later...

Ted, rightly, suspects that John is the decision-maker, because when all is going well, he glances around, offering relaxed smiles. But when they reach a sticky area, or if he is disappointed with someone's performance, he drops his eyes towards the table and avoids eye contact with any of his team. In effect, he's left the meeting in order to contemplate the consequences. Another sign might be quickly handling something on the table, such as a glass of water. His team then slows down, as if to give him time to think things through.

3 Coffee break

Ted tells his team that when Magnastruct proposed a deposit of 10 per cent of the total cost before starting work, John did not look away or down, and that his pupils became very dilated, and that he moved forward in his seat (above). He also blinked several times in succession: in other contexts, this would probably have meant disbelief, but here it meant simply pleasant surprise. Ted bets that Baker were probably expecting to pay a much larger deposit.

Group negotiations

4 Crunch time

Below, the timing of the final payment is being discussed. Magnastruct wants it all paid when they finish work, with a clause in the contract obliging them to sort out, at no further cost, teething problems occurring up to six months after the completion date.

Ted notices that during this exchange, John and others in the Baker team move very slightly away from the table and avoid eye contact with each other, suggesting that they discussed the issue in detail before negotiations began and were resolute that no final payment should be made until the plant was fully commissioned, and up and running.

Over lunch, Ted tells his team that he does not believe Baker will move on this issue, and that they had best try to compensate by asking for a larger deposit.

5 After lunch

Baker's negotiators are still adamant about the final payment, and seem to be trying to wear down Magnastruct's team by introducing a non-essential discussion about inspecting the work. One of the team even stops paying attention for a moment. Magnastruct's team now wearily try to overcome the problem of the timing of payments again, saying that if the final tranche is to be withheld until the plant is running, the deposit would have to be 40 per cent.

6 'Just as I thought'

Ted notices that the muscles around John's mouth are tightening (above). His eyes and head tilt slightly upwards with a hint of irony, and he takes a deep breath: all indicators that this move was exactly as he had anticipated. The Baker team's chief executive explains that 40 per cent is unrealistic and offers 30 per cent. Baker appears to stick on this position, but Ted has advised his team to tough it out at 40 per cent because he's so sure that Baker were expecting all along to pay as much as that up front.

Soon John has moved forwards towards the table, his hands are open and facing upwards and his main negotiator is throwing sideways glances at him: all of which are signs that John is eager to wrap it up and get the contract signed on the basis of 40 per cent as an advance payment and the final payment when the plant is fully commissioned.

Interviews are artificial situations: short, intense periods of acquaintance that can lead to long-term commitments on both sides. Naturally, interviewees want to present themselves at their best, and the skilful ones are quite capable of pretending that they are whatever the interviewer wants them to be – regardless of whether or not they are in fact remotely suitable for the job. Conversely, the best candidate might come across poorly in interviews.

As an interviewer, it's essential that you should be able to cut through the persona to the person beneath, and the most effective way to do this is to make your questions work hand in hand with your knowledge of body language.

As an interviewee, you must learn to communicate positive messages about yourself by the cultivation of good body language – and, of course, to avoid creating negative impressions by constantly monitoring yourself for bad body language.

Whichever side of the desk you are going to be sitting on, this short chapter offers a few pointers.

You might imagine that getting a job is about having the right combination of experience, skills and personal attributes – and in part it is. But it's also about how you 'come across' in interviews – much of which is down to your body language. If your actions and gestures convey a relaxed confidence, you are already ahead of the game.

Interviewing

Interview checklist

Time and again in this book I've warned against the dangers of viewing body language in isolation (see page 14). Having said that, there are occasions when, whether you like it or not, your body language *will* be viewed in isolation: interviews are perhaps the commonest example. When you are interviewed for a job, your body language will be judged by a total stranger who may well know little or nothing about its meaning, so it is important to avoid giving negative signals inadvertently.

Preparation

With this in mind, I've devised the following checklists of good and bad body language to provide a pre-interview crash course. Read and digest them; make yourself aware of how you will or will not be judged for your body language at interview, for reasons right or wrong; and after the interview, forget all about it.

Good body language

The following types of body language tend, whether rightly or wrongly, to create good first impressions:

- A positive entrance
- Smiling in a relaxed manner
- Making eye contact
- A firm handshake
- Use of hand gestures to support what you are saying
- Maintaining an erect posture
- When seated, leaning forward slightly to convey attentiveness

Unbuttoned

Consider little details like buttoning
and unbuttoning your jacket (left). Does it
look too informal to have your jacket
unbuttoned when you are standing or
walking? And when you are seated, does
staying buttoned make you look uptight?
Watch how television presenters
continually button and unbutton their
jackets when sitting or standing. It's
a habit worth acquiring.

Ready to go

Lean forwards in your chair – chin up,
but not too far. Keep the tips of your fingers
together, in your lap, pointing forwards, not
up or down. Do this and you will send the
message: 'I am confident enough to want to
get straight into the interview.' Be careful,
though: if overdone, as here (right), this
approach might put the interviewer on the
defensive, or even seem threatening.

Interview checklist

Hands locked defensively across midriff, pleading expression

Smoking

Biting pens or other objects

Fidgeting hands, running fingers through hair

Bad body language

The different types of body language illustrated above all send the same message: 'I'm nervous' – as do the following:

- Whistling
- Jiggling contents of pocket
- Clearing throat
- Hand-wringing
- Clicking tongue

Arms crossed in front of chest

Chin down

Tight-lipped grin

Frowning

Above, the common message is 'I'm unsure'. The same applies to:
- Squinting
- Pulling away
- Touching nose or face
- Darting eye movements
- Pointing with fingers
- Rubbing back of neck
- Chopping one hand into palm of the other

The interview

Alice really wants this job. She's been unable to relax for days before the interview. The interviewer, John, cannot know this. All he sees is that Alice presents herself at the interview in a tense, anxious state.

John's problem is to decide how much Alice's body language arises from an understandable nervousness about the interview process, and how much from defensiveness – a desire to cover up weaknesses. If John gives her too hard a time, the chances are that he'll learn even less of the truth than he otherwise would do.

John   Alice

1 Nervous start

Alice (above) looks tense and defensive. Her upright position, with legs tucked under the seat, arms straight, and hands clasped between her legs, are all body language trouble spots. There is no way of telling at this stage whether she is merely nervous or has things to hide. John's only option is to be patient and to let her unwind in her own time. Note the position of Alice's feet (left). They have now moved forward slightly, but even so, they are still nervously tight to the chair.

2 Settling down?

John's training as an interviewer has taught him to do the obvious in a situation like this (see right). He gives Alice some background about what sort of company she's hoping to join, bringing in anecdotes from the last sales conference, with one or two designed to make her laugh. He hands her a brochure that illustrates a point he's making, so that in receiving it, she has to move forward. Just a small gesture such as this can speed the calming process when someone is genuinely nervous. John should now be looking to see if Alice's feet come involuntarily forward from under the seat. If so, this would confirm that she's starting to settle down.

3 Going better

Some minutes later, Alice has realized that the interview is less frightening than she had expected (see left). Her body language has softened accordingly. The arms are no longer forming a tight defensive barrier and the feet have strayed out from under the chair. There is even some mirroring behaviour: Alice is unconsciously echoing John's crossed legs and pointing foot (see page 35). So far so good. There seems to be little doubt that her tight body language was just down to nervousness. But now turn to the next page.

The interview

4 Talking turkey

Once John has seen Alice's body language starting to soften, he uses the standard interviewing technique of mixing questions that will help him assess how Alice has succeeded in her current job, and how she would cope in the new position.

John now starts to ask some specific questions. He wants to know what Alice did to improve the credit control system she worked on and how she measured her effect. The question seems to touch a raw nerve: Alice's legs move backwards, the head drops a little and the hands are folded into a tighter barrier, all suggesting defensiveness and concealment.

John needs to know exactly why she is feeling uncomfortable, but wisely accepts that having invested so much time getting Alice to open up, it would be self-defeating to press the point.

John now asks Alice to tell him what she thinks were her best achievements in running her department. Again the feet drift forwards and the hands loosen up. Having heard Alice's answer, John decides quite quickly that she'll be OK for the post and hints at this, without saying it directly. Before Alice's body language can change, however, he reverts to the credit control question, asking her what part she played and how she felt about it.

5 Flashback

Alice is biting her bottom lip and stroking her chin – both gestures indicating that she's trying to make up her mind about what to say. As she explains how poorly the project was handled, and how she had disagreed with the results, John is pleased to see that her pupils are slightly raised and that they are moving from left to right and back again. This is typical of people who are recalling events as they actually happened – their eyes are 'seeing' the events as pictures that go with the words. She is confirming her own story as she relates it.

Broadly speaking, right-handed people's pupils have a tendency to move from left to right when they are recalling events as they happened; left-hander's pupils move right to left.

6 Home straight

John now says, 'Well, I can understand why you're looking for a new job – seems a sensible move to me.' Alice's body language again opens up, confirming that she's at ease with the situation, and with John's opinion of her. Her body language is closely mirroring John's – particularly the position of the hands, first in the lap, then extending forward towards the knee. These are strong signs that she approves of John because she feels he has assessed her fairly.

This chapter looks at ways of coping with the personality clashes that can arise within the office environment – whether because of the arrogance of a colleague, office politics or for some other reason. I offer tips on how to reduce the effectiveness of intimidating gestures such as stiff handshakes and hard stares. I also look at the pitfalls inherent in being a boss in the modern age, where there is a constant balancing act between inspiring and challenging your staff on the one hand, and maintaining authority and distance on the other. Go too far in one direction, and you may create an over-familiarity that can undermine your own position; too far in the other, and you run the risk of alienating your workforce.

No office is a conflict-free zone. Often it's the survival of the fittest, as colleagues compete, dispute, undermine and jostle for position. To survive and flourish in the world of work, you must be equipped to deal with difficult situations – and difficult people. Understanding their body language is the first step.

Being assertive

Regaining the status quo

It is highly unlikely that you will go through the whole of your working life without encountering aggression, confrontation, power play and all the other varieties of human behaviour that make life so colourful – especially since the workplace is, by definition, the place where we interact on a daily basis with total strangers, or at least with people whom we have not chosen to be our friends or acquaintances.

The body language in this section is all about asserting your right to deal with other people on level terms, something you have to do when you are confronted by a domineering colleague, or by anyone who is over-confident, arrogant or just plain awkward.

It will often be perfectly obvious when your position is under threat. Sometimes, however, territorial infringements can be subtle: if someone leans on your desk, for instance, it can undermine your authority. The means of counteracting such infringements are equally subtle.

First, a word of caution: these techniques will get you nowhere if you're trying to gain the advantage with a tough negotiator. (Instead, use the very different but equally effective body language discussed on pages 66–71.)

Recognizing difficult types

Next we look at three common types of 'difficult' personality: the dominant male, the know-it-all, and the bone crusher.

The dominant male
Arms folded in combination with a stiff body, leaning back: a posture typical of the highly dominant, objective-driven type.

The know-it-all
Hands steepled upwards, betraying someone who 'knows it all'. It's a particularly common gesture among lawyers and accountants.

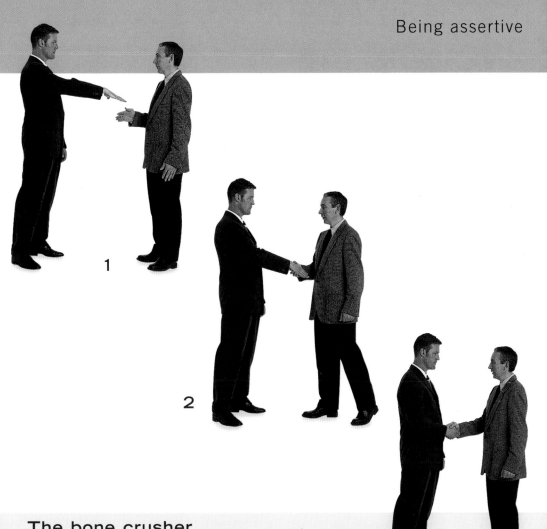

The bone crusher

Dominant types like to use a stiff-armed, palm-downwards handshake, fixing you with an unwavering downwards gaze (1). To counter this, move forwards with your right foot as you take the shake, making a short, surprise raid into your aggressor's social territory zone. At the same time, try to bring the handshake into a horizontal position, if possible with your hand above his, to raise it almost back to the level where he started it. The shake is now neutralized (3). The bone-crusher is disconcerted by the raid on his personal space, not least because there's nothing he can do, or say, about it.

Bull's eye

You can deal with the downward gaze in the scenario on the previous page by looking steadily back into the area shown by the triangle in the illustration above. This 'business gaze' creates a serious atmosphere and warns the other person that you are not playing about. Provided your gaze doesn't drop below their eye level you will maintain this status quo, and thus a measure of control. When the gaze drops below eye level, a social atmosphere develops (see pages 34–35), and your opponent may well try to regain the initiative by making boastful or 'one-up' statements.

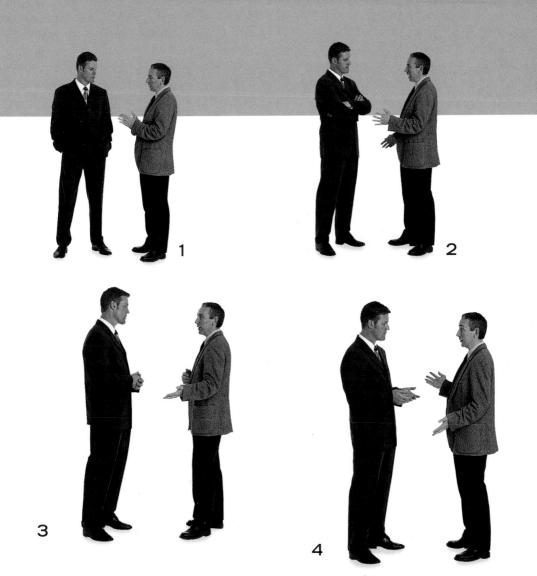

Don't get mad, get even

Go to a party and observe people who like each other, or agree on a topic: you will see that they unconsciously copy each other's gestures. This sends the unspoken message, 'I'm in tune with you; we can communicate.' In a face-to-face encounter, you can use your own body language to fool a difficult colleague into a relaxed and receptive frame of mind. First ignore his negative gestures (1 and 2) and begin to adopt unhurried, positive body language with plenty of eye contact. This should gradually soften his negative gestures (3 and 4).

Assertive or aggressive?

If you have recently been promoted and, as is presumably the case, you want to stay in charge, you would be well advised to unlearn the body language shown on the following pages. In the past, you may have seen your superiors adopting poses like these, and perhaps you asked yourself how they could possibly believe in the effectiveness of such clichéd power plays. Sadly, these types of body language come all too easily to those who feel insecure with their new-found authority. They can seem like useful props for dealing with an insolently questioning subordinate or a challenging whizz kid, but in the long run they will do nothing to enhance your authority.

Aggressive

If you have a good point and can argue it effectively, it should speak for itself; there should be no need to underline it by leaning forwards aggressively as you speak (above). Avoid finger-pointing: far from being a sign of authority, it suggests that you are losing control of the situation, and smacks, if anything, of playground gun-play.

Remote

You may think that keeping people 'at arm's length' (above) – in your work area, at the coffee machine, wherever – is an effective way of marking a change in status by increasing the size of your personal zone (see page 18). In fact, it's one of the oldest ploys in the book, and usually seen as such.

Superior

Looking down your nose (above) is *the* oldest ploy in the book. The merest backwards tilt of the head is enough to convey a message of not-so-subtle assumed superiority. Far from gaining the respect of your subordinates, such behaviour is more likely to make you an object of ridicule.

Assertive or aggressive?

Very busy

There are few things more irritating than going for a meeting with your boss and being kept waiting outside his office. The only thing worse is to be kept waiting again once you are inside, while the big man carries on with his work (above) as if you didn't exist. Don't inflict this on your co-workers.

Manipulative

Exaggerating any of your gestures can amount to power play – as if the person you address is too stupid to understand them otherwise. The same goes for excessive touching (they are so lowly they need extra reassurance), and for other signs of condescension such as excessive eye contact or a sugary tone.

Plain nasty

This kind of boss turns away when someone else talks, or perhaps makes little snorting gestures to put them off their stride. He struts around as if he owns it all – a sure sign that he doesn't. His gaze may be expressionless, angry or staring; his body tense, with hands on hips, head tilted sideways and narrowed eyes.

Spec-ulative

In the wrong hands, even spectacles can become a tool of power play. While a subordinate is making a point, the boss slowly removes his glasses and cleans them, or perhaps blows away some imaginary dust. Then he puts them back on unhurriedly, gazing at his victim all the while.

95

Communicating status

It can seem unfair that some people in authority seem to have positive body language apparently without trying. These people are often described as charismatic: everyone is seemingly aware of them as they enter the room; they give off an 'aura'; they are 'listened to'; they only have to smile and people 'light up'; people want to follow them. President Clinton is perhaps the most often-quoted example of such a person.

There may well be such a thing as charisma, but I suspect that much of it is in the eye of the beholder, rather than down to any special technique. If you are completely comfortable in a leadership role and if your leadership qualities are based on an unselfish desire to empower colleagues to do their work better, rather than simply to dominate for its own sake, then I think it follows that people will sense you are on their side.

Seeming certain

At your desk or at a meeting table, press your palms firmly downwards on to the surface to communicate certainty. Do this when you really feel sure about what you are saying; do it instead of finger-pointing or other flamboyant hand gestures to underline points. It's more expressive than you think, and it steadies you as you speak.

Rewarding, not dominating

Expressing appreciation of good work is a fundamental tool for managers seeking to motivate people. There are many ways to do this – spoken and written. Nicely judged body language can be a powerful back-up to spoken appreciation.

Hold the handshake fractionally longer as you say, 'Well done'. Lightly touch a shoulder as you say, 'That turned out well' (right). Do this only when you really feel sincere about congratulating someone. If you do it to turn a half-hearted compliment into what you hope will appear to be a 'bigger' one, the body language could well seem phoney and manipulative to the recipient.

Communicating status

If you have been recently promoted into a senior position – perhaps even the most senior position of all – there are a number of ways to communicate your new status positively.

John

Straight down the line

This one is obvious, but still worth thinking about. When facing a subordinate, try to make your stance upright, but don't pull yourself up or try to 'tower' Keep the torso straight on, not angled; use an open smile. These three gestures in combination, shown above by John, are very positive.

In touch

After a few moments, he steeples his hands with fingers pointing towards her, arms raised. This says 'I'm sceptical about what you are saying' or even, 'I feel superior'. Hands steepled towards her, but with arms lower, would mean 'I'm not only listening, but I'm in touch'.

When you walk

Be upright and relaxed (right). Let the silent voice inside your head say: 'I know this place back to front', not 'I own it, top to bottom'.

Being sensitive to submissive gestures

Watch for:

- Fidgeting, fiddling
- Covering mouth and eyes
- Poor eye contact
- Eyes closing briefly
- Imitating too many of your gestures
- Slumped posture
- Quiet, faltering voice
- Pleading smile
- Body lowering

These can be marked signs of submission. If you start seeing them in clusters, over a period of minutes, then ask yourself if your body language is too dominant. Are you making the subordinate feel small and nervous? Subordinates should feel alert but relaxed in your presence. Maybe you're looking down your nose? (For other negative forms of power play, see pages 92–95.)

Unhurried gestures

Submissive people have speedy, jerky gestures. Dominant people are the opposite. When you're newly promoted, unhurried gestures may not be habitual, so there is no harm in telling yourself to slow everything down a little. But don't force it. If it feels unnatural, it will look phoney.

Dealing with difficult people

When to cut your losses

The body language sequence on these two pages is a no-win situation for those unfortunate enough to come up against it. Taken in isolation, each of these gestures is bad enough. Flowing one from another, they are extremely depressing. Your best option is to listen neutrally, and get out at the first opportunity.

1 Pulling rank

Chris, as usual, is using office furniture power-play to give himself an advantage. But today this is worsened by an additional problem: he's in his 'rank has its privileges' mood.

Chris

2 The good old days

Chris is explaining how he would like things done, how they have always been done, and how successfully they have been done that way. As he speaks, he moves back in his chair and talks to the ceiling – not to Alice. This combination of body language means extreme arrogance and self-assurance. Alice would be wisest not to respond: he won't hear.

3 Why are you telling me this?

Alice now ventures a brief comment. Chris's finger-up-the-cheek gesture means that he is not even remotely interested in what she's saying.

4 Live to fight another day

Alice's best option is to make this meeting as short as she possibly can. She could make use of silence in the brief intervals between his speech, followed by a non-committal 'Right' or 'I see'. If she rushes out a response as he tails off, Chris will take it as confirmation of his dominance. Then she should go away and respond on paper, if necessary getting the support of colleagues.

Alice

Dealing with difficult people

In this scenario, Alice wants something from Chris, namely a pay rise and extra responsibility. Chris is unable to give it. He also knows, from previous meetings, that Alice can become very difficult on these occasions – not only high-handed, but threatening as well. Meetings have ended in a bad atmosphere and Alice has been unbearable and unproductive for weeks afterwards. Chris wants to pre-empt this situation by starting in charge and staying in charge – but without arguing.

I Setting the scene

Chris has given himself an advantage by holding the meeting in his office. He's made sure that the base of his chair is slightly higher than Alice's, putting her in a body-lower position (below). He is also sitting right opposite her, closer in than the business zone but still well outside of the intimate zone (see page 19), giving the appearance of accessibility while actually maintaining some distance. The unspoken message is, 'We are here for business, and feelings shouldn't come into it.' Alice will find it difficult to take control.

Chris

Alice

2 Taking control

Chris is still well in control. Even though his body is partly shielded by the arms, by leaning backwards he exposes it square-on to Alice, sending the message that he feels secure in his dominance (right).

If Alice wants to get out of this, she needs to find an excuse to meet again later, preferably on more neutral territory. She needs to appear cooperative, but in reality try to wear him down.

3 Maintaining your position

Chris can enhance his feeling of control by occasionally looking over the top of his glasses (left), accentuating the effect of looking down from a height, and so of making Alice feel that she's in a lower, subordinate position. His eyes should be either on the bull's eye zone (see page 90) or maintain direct contact with Alice's. This sends the message, 'I am not nervous of you or this situation.'

Truth is a precious commodity, and I've no wish to downgrade it. There's no denying, however, that in the workplace being economic with the truth is a day-to-day necessity. Sometimes, telling the truth can even be illegal: for instance when a company is in secret talks to purchase another, and stock market prices could be affected if the news got out. At others, it's just not expedient: admitting that you're trying to find a new location for your organization, far away from the present one, could compromise everyone's livelihood until the issue is sorted out.

If you have to lie, make sure you do it as well as possible. This section starts with a couple of pages to make you aware of other people's body language when you're being less than straightforward. Then it goes on to describe the art of lying well.

Doubt, disbelief and lies

Doubt and disbelief

These two pages are about recognizing when someone else thinks you're lying. (To discover how best to mask your own untruths, see pages 110–113.)

In our scenario, Alex is telling his subordinate, Bob, how he wants a project handled. He begins by exaggerating the amount of money available, and then goes on to lie about how long the work will take.

There's no need for Bob to articulate his disbelief: his body does it for him.

Bob

Alex

1 Oh really?

Look at Bob's reaction (above). The combination of leaning back with legs crossed and arms folded indicates that he is experiencing mild doubt. (Don't confuse this body language with that shown on page 24 for someone who has lost interest, or has become disappointed in what they are hearing.) The two types are broadly similar, but the key difference is that here the head is neither tilted down, nor is it supported.

2 Cold shoulder

If Bob's initial body language is followed by the slight turning away of a shoulder (below), it probably indicates that his mild doubt is now beginning to turn into boredom.

Hand-to-face gestures

All body language needs to be understood in context – particularly hand-to-face gestures. In isolation, you can be fairly confident that they indicate the listener has had a negative thought; the difficulty is in assessing just *how* negative? Sometimes, such gestures simply display a private and passing worry or apprehension, but as a development from the body language observed on the opposite page, Bob's hand-to-face movement (left) is much more likely to betray disbelief. On the following pages, these movements become increasingly restless as Bob's discomfort becomes more and more visible to the observer.

3 See no evil

Now Alex takes Bob by surprise with a wildly over-optimistic business forecast. Bob's response is shown right: a series of very rapid blinks, lasting perhaps less than a second, showing that Bob can't quite take in what he's hearing. This is hard to spot without practice, and always easiest to see if the person observed faces into the light.

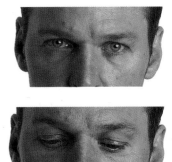

Doubt and disbelief

4 Hear no evil

Alex now tells a string of blatant lies. Bob reacts by making quick rubbing movements to the area below the eye, to the forehead and then to an earlobe (right). He might also rub his nose, cover his mouth, or pull at his collar (below right). These gestures help to dissipate an almost imperceptible pricking sensation or discomfort caused by blood coming to the surface of the skin, or possibly by increased sweating. These are physical responses to Bob's internal conflict between between being polite to his boss and not believing what he says. Touching the earlobes sends the message, 'I don't want to hear this.'

   These expressions have been deliberately exaggerated to make the body language clear. In reality, they are of course much more subtle and fleeting, and almost impossible to capture on film.

5 Facing facts

When the time comes to look Alex in the face, Bob's eyes will probably be slightly more narrowed than usual. The unspoken message is, 'I don't want to see what I see.'

Congruence

Congruence (see also page 23) plays a key role when you are trying to detect a liar, or when you want to suppress your own lies. The liar might hold out his hands in a 'believe me' gesture, but give himself away by a contradictory signal such as being unable to maintain eye contact; or he may simply try too hard. For example, who would you suspect: someone who avoids eye contact, or someone who fixes the gaze for too long?

109

How to lie well

Lying isn't easy. When you lie, all sorts of uncontrollable signals are activated by the autonomic nervous system: blushing, sweating palms, dry mouth, tickly nose and throat. Hiding such signals is an art in itself, and takes much practice. Untrained liars may be revealed by the abnormality of their speech patterns: for instance, slowed speech, delayed responses and a general lack of spontaneity. They may also avoid using the first person, as if they are trying to disown the deceit. More practised liars will know more tricks.

As most people know, the best way to lie is to stick to as many elements of the truth as possible, so that the signs of lying are minimized and it is easier to remain consistent. The smaller the lie, the more likely it is to be effective.

The worst liars are those who try to convince their audience of the accuracy of their statements by the use of certain body language signals, which they mistakenly believe convey an impression of honesty.

Basic mistake no. 1

Deliberately looking someone in the eye. **As a child, you were doubtless challenged many times, 'Look me in the eye and tell me that again.' Children, teenagers and young adults do tend to look away when telling less than the truth. It's natural to believe that by looking someone in the eye, you'll reinforce the impression of honesty. But anyone with a little understanding of body language will be suspicious of this, especially if you compound the mistake by not blinking.**

The right way

Try to be aware of looking into the face rather than the pupils, as below. In reality, you won't be able to avoid looking into the pupils completely, but try to do it for no more than 75 per cent of the time.

Basic mistake no. 2

Changes in voice. When you lie, your voice tends to go flat – you think that by controlling pitch and resonance, you'll sound more convincing. Not true. Coupled with a steady look into the listener's eyes, a change in normal voice modulation often means lies.

The right way
Tell yourself to keep talking with as many as possible of your usual 'ups' and 'downs'.

Basic mistake no. 3

Body more rigid than usual, whether sitting or standing. It's as if the body is stiffening with the effort of concealment.

The right way
Difficult to advise, because an individual's 'normal' posture is so variable. If you are an especially animated person, make an extra effort to 'hang loose'.

Basic mistake no. 4

Fidgeting with hands and arms. One second, the hands are hidden behind the back; next, they dive into the pockets; next,

they're visible, but clasping the arms, palms turned in; next, one hand is hidden. These activities are even more indicative if combined, as above, with hand-to-face gestures – such a sequence is often repeated several times while lies are being told. (See also page 113 for more on the role of palms when lying or telling the truth.)

The right way
Keep the hands still, moving them only when you need to. If they are clasped together, it might look as if you're trying too hard, so keep them apart, and any gestures understated.

How to lie well

Politicians and lawyers are among the best liars: their main technique is to neutralize their body language, rendering their gestures neither positive nor negative.

The skilful politicians have a knack of talking and acting in a manner seemingly unique to them: assured, authoritative, unemotional, never lost for words. To do this, they employ a low vocal monotone with the minimum of head and body movement. Remove the words, and every such speaker would make the same basic sounds, with the same body language – it's the same performance, regardless of script.

More on hand-to-face gestures

It's not only the listener who experiences involuntary tingling or facial itching when lies are told; the liar does too. These types of movement are real give-aways, easy to spot, but they're also easy to avoid: just tell yourself to leave the offending areas alone. Above are three more face-rubbing gestures that give the lie to the liar.

Palm gestures

Palms tell all. Open palms symbolize openness and sincerity; palms open facing upwards say, 'I'm bearing all' (left). It is something we do instinctively, and just as instinctively, we trust others who do it.

Palms hidden are a sign of deceit, but as always, be aware of body language working in clusters. Merely exposing your palms will not necessarily convince people that you are telling the truth. You may overlook other 'lying' gestures which will contradict your open palms, as will the lack of other supporting 'truth' gestures, adding up to a non-convincing cluster.

Accomplished liars are well aware of this: they use palm-up gestures sparingly, knowing that if they are combined with other, contradictory body language, such as stiff posture or a flattened voice, listeners will be suspicious. The experienced liar will try to hide as much of his body as possible behind a desk, and use occasional palm-up gestures to reinforce key points.

Constricting pupils

Even the best liars in the world cannot stop their pupils constricting when they lie. If possible, keep your face out of the light, so your pupils are hard to see. Skilled negotiators often try to arrange seating so they can see into your eyes but you can't see into theirs.

113

The working day may seem to be over, but sometimes you find you're still on duty: business dinners, receptions, gatherings of any sort, including the office party, are of course all part of working life – and how you come across on 'social occasions' can affect your career.

You can get ahead of the game by learning to read body language that reveals whether people like you on a social level – or indeed whether they're attracted to you.

Let's be honest, the presence, or the absence, of a sexual undercurrent in an after-hours encounter could be relevant to the way you should play it when you meet next day in a work situation.

After hours

Questions of status

John   Vanessa

Arriving at a function you often find yourself in the awkward situation of being in the company of some interesting or high-status person on whom you'd like to make your mark. The trouble is that you don't know whether to seize the moment now while you have them to yourself, or to manoeuvre for their attention inside, against competiton from all and sundry. Here's how to make up your mind by reading their body language.

1 Cool it

As Vanessa says 'Hello' (above), she should watch the way John's body is pointing. If his head swivels towards her but his trunk keeps pointing through the door towards the party, it probably means he is more interested in getting into the room than pausing to talk to her. If his body swivels towards Vanessa, however, he may well be receptive to an advance.

2 Still cautious

John politely acknowledges Vanessa, but he has not engaged. His feet point away, even though his body is half turned towards her. She must resist moving in quickly, but keep to her territory and avoid facing him directly.

3 Watch the zone

John, Vanessa's new boss, has turned his trunk directly towards Vanessa and both of his feet are pointing at her. This is good, but at this stage Vanessa should stay firmly on the edge of the business zone (see page 18) in order not to seem pushy so early in the encounter.

4 Close in a little

Only if John gets talking should Vanessa edge in a little in order to get good eye contact (see page 34).

117

Body and foot pointing

The body language on these two pages generally amounts to more open and obvious – that is, social – versions of what you've seen already (see pages 46 and 72).

1 Formations
At social functions, it can be interesting to watch the angles at which people stand in relation to each other. In Western countries, particularly in the English-speaking world, people who aren't intimate tend to stand at about 90 degrees to each other while socializing (above). The chances are that they'll be discussing a general topic.

2 Closing
If the angle starts getting narrower, they may be moving on to a more confidential or personal issue.

3 Two's company
While the angle was about 90 degrees, they would probably have been happy if a third had joined them; if it narrows, the arrival of a third wouldn't be so welcome.

4 Up close and personal

If the conversation becomes personal and entertaining, you are likely to see closed formations like those shown above and below.

Smokers' signals

Reading these is very much a matter of common sense – they're highly indicative of a smoker's inner state because of course much of the value of cigarettes, pipes and cigars to smokers is the release of tension and stress. Those who don't smoke instead resort to general grooming rituals such as nail biting, finger and foot tapping, adjusting their cufflinks and compulsively drinking.

It's probably true that blowing smoke upwards is a sign of a confident and positive mood; blowing smoke downwards means the opposite, perhaps also a secretive and supicious frame of mind. A card-player dealt a good hand is more likely to blow smoke upwards than downwards, and vice-versa.

Traditionally, long, fat cigars emphasize status, but these days it's probably more useful to know that cigar smoking and connoisseurship have been very much on the increase, especially in the USA. Afficionados may well choose a small-sized cigar from a top-quality brand.

Body and foot pointing

When seated

John is sending the unspoken message that he wants to ask Ted a direct, personal question (right). If Ted is a subordinate, he'll get the message that John could be about to put him on the spot. A more subtle way to manage this scenario is for John to sit at a right angle and then broach the tricky issue informally (below).

John

John should watch Ted for hand-to-face gestures (see page 112) as he makes his response (below): they can indicate the frankness – or otherwise – of the reply.

Wanted or unwanted?

Alice and Betsy have been talking. Ted joins them. If Alice's and Betsy's feet start rotating to point at Ted, even when they are still talking to each other, then it's likely that they not only accept Ted, but appreciate his presence (below). Women are far more sensitive to body language in these – and most other situations – than men. If you're a man, and in doubt about how to behave in an encounter such as this, trust the way the women play it.

Alice

Betsy

Here you see a man who is both welcome and unwelcome. His upright posture, arm on table and hand on knee suggest he is staying only briefly at the table. Whilst the girl in the centre is interested in what he is saying, the girl on the left has moved away from the table and crossed her legs, with raised foot pointing away. She is being polite but doesn't feel part of the conversation or doesn't want to get involved. Either way, she would prefer him to leave.

Making the wheels go round

These two pages cover a miscellany of easy-to-use and easy-to-remember body language designed to help you be more at ease with people socially and to improve the quality of your communication.

Sincere and insincere smiles

Experts say that sincere smiles (left) build gradually, then fade gradually, both sides of the face tending to smile to the same degree – with a symmetrical, rounded effect. An insincere smile (below) tends to last unnaturally long, may look asymmetrical, and ends suddenly. A nervous, insecure smile tends to last less long than it should, and to cut off suddenly.

Artful positioning

As we have seen, there are three territorial zones – intimate, social and business (see page 18). When people first meet at a social function, they prefer to be on the outer limits of the social zone, and it's almost always a mistake to push in closer during the opening rounds of conversation; at this stage, avoid the temptation to try to impress by leaning close to someone's ear and muttering an amusingly indiscreet comment about a fellow guest.

However, after a minute or two, you could try edging a little closer, watching carefully for their reaction. If the other person makes none, or backs off, leave it at that. If they edge fractionally closer too, this is a sign that you're communicating well and that they probably want to continue talking.

Warm, but not threatening

Men who feel the urge to be 'touchy feely' early on in an encounter with a woman they find attractive and would like to impress should – as a general rule – overcome the urge and look for the female's unspoken invitation instead (see page 130). On the whole, the most a man should venture in

the early stages is a quick touch on the arm, expressing warmth without being overtly sexual (above); women tend to appreciate this gesture. Of course, there are many exceptions to this rule. Some girls like the bold but lighthearted approach – arm straight around the shoulders, hovering close to the breast on the far side – but these tactics are self-defeating unless the male also knows how to read the 'stop, that's too much too soon' signals.

Going well

Ted has correctly read Vanessa's positive body language and nicely timed his quick raid into her personal zone to tell her a joke about a colleague (above).

123

Making the wheels go round

Circling around

Don't be disconcerted if you notice a male and a female circling around each other at a social gathering in a somewhat aggressive way. Restless changing of position can be a sign of mutual attraction and appraisal, possibly serving to provide a changing array of visual stimuli. If it is accompanied by repartee – part slightly challenging, even unfriendly, part joking – possibly also by smiles and stares, you may well be witnessing the start of a relationship. Sexual attraction has an aggressive element, which is sometimes carefully hidden, sometimes near the surface.

Starting well

Mirroring has cropped up earlier in this book (see, for example, Cloning the boss page 48), and here it is (right) in one of its most positive forms, at the start of a new friendship. Clare's and Alice's torsos both point at the same diagonal angle, the necks have the same amount of twist, the heads are held almost at the same height. They both like each other and are very comfortable with the way things are going.

Clare   Alice

Nods and smiles

It's easy to forget that nodding or smiling in the pauses in someone's conversation helps them to talk better, so remind yourself of this before meeting people. It also gives you a measure of control over the conversation; they'll see you as a good listener, and feel keen to please, which in turn makes it easier for you to steer them towards topics you're interested in.

125

Men attracting women

What do men do to attract the opposite sex? The truthful answer is: compared with women, not much. Male courtship gestures are not only limited, they are clumsy and crude compared with the average female's weaponry.

Stomach in, chest out

In the presence of a woman he finds attractive, a man tends to assume an erect posture (right). The sagging belly is eliminated (as far as possible); to help with this, the chest is thrust out. It may be that this emphasis on the chest serves to accentuate the triangular torso shape that women find attractive in men (just as men respond to the hour-glass shape of women).

Holding the gaze

Sophisticated males, with some grasp of, and ability to read body language, are most likely to rely on their gaze to send signals, rather than cruder physical gestures. Women are usually conscious of men's eyes moving up and down between the face and pelvic region, with frequent pauses in the area of the breasts – even if they've just met. An especially interested male will move beyond this quite quickly to engineer a meeting of the eyes at every opportunity. The length of time this gaze is held – often measured in fractions of a second – tells a woman much about the extent of the man's interest, and his self-confidence.

Preening

Straightening the tie, brushing dust –
real or imaginary – from clothes, and
smoothing the hair are all gestures which
hark back to man's primitive past.
Indeed, studies of monkey groups
highlight the fact that the dominant,
most sexually active male is the sleekest
and best groomed.

Ready to go

This is about as obvious as male body
language can be: a combination of the
crude and familiar 'I'm ready to go'
gesture with a positioning of the hands
centrally, tucked into the belt, to
accentuate the genital region. Thanks to
Westerns, it's a cliché, and to be honest,
you don't see it much, except in young
males. But elder males often display a
toned-down, hands-on-hips version,
pointing the torso directly at the woman.
This may be combined with holding the
intimate gaze a few seconds longer than
the norm. Dilated pupils tell the female
that he's subconsciously interested.

Men attracting women

Following her around

Men will follow an especially interesting female around the room with their eyes. Women often sense that a man's eyes are on them, even when their back is turned. When a woman describes a romantic encounter in terms of 'eyes meeting across a room', what she may well be saying is that, having noticed his gaze upon her for some time, she then 'accidentally' allows her eyes to 'find' this gaze. There is some research to show that women will do this when it suits them, rather than respond 'on demand'.

All in good time

The reverse can also be true: women do sneak frequent glances at men they find attractive, but they are generally subtler and harder to spot. It's as if women use their expertise in body language to give themselves time to make up their minds. Men commonly describe progress towards intimacy with a girl as if it's on the female's timetable, not theirs.

Take a look at this...

Standing against a wall often facilitates a subtle (or not-so-subtle) forward tilt of the pelvis which most women will recognize without difficulty.

... or this

Some men may sit legs-apart in a blatant crotch display (right).

In with a chance

Here's a good example of positive male body language towards a woman. His stance is confident, but not overbearing. The torso is presented face-on, but it's held loosely and he meets her gaze directly, but not cheekily, or for too long. He doesn't grip her hand too long, either, and even if he's interested, he's careful not to make any fresh moves too suddenly.

A large number of women – but by no means all – find this combination of body language attractive and easy to deal with. It says 'I might well be interested, but I'm not forcing myself on you; the next move is yours.' Women appreciate a warm, open, but unhurried attitude – as I've said elsewhere, they tend to have their own timetable for moving towards intimacy. It's best to let them follow it – after all, they're the body language experts.

Women attracting men

Women use the same basic signalling gestures as men: hands on hips to draw attention to the body shape or to the pelvic area; smoothing the clothing; hair touching; foot and body pointing in the direction of the man they find attractive; holding the gaze (see page 126). All of these are familiar female courtship gestures, as is the hip-roll when walking, again to draw attention to the pelvic region. However, as you'll see on these pages, gaze behaviour is far more diverse. Pupil dilation is a giveaway, if you can spot it, as is colouring of the cheeks.

But there's plenty more ...

Glancing sideways

The man's gaze is held only long enough for him to notice, then she looks away. She may look at him 'through her eyelashes' – she drops her head and steals an upward glance through slightly lowered lids. The message is 'I'm looking at you, but not long enough for you to know exactly what it means. You'll have to find out more.' This can drive some men wild.

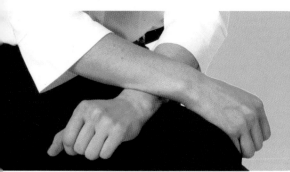

Ambiguous gestures

Left, hiding the wrists may be a courtship gesture – it's hard to tell. Some experts think that if a girl lets a male see the skin of her wrists by degrees, then it may be an invitation. Girls also know how to 'fix' a man with a momentary, direct,

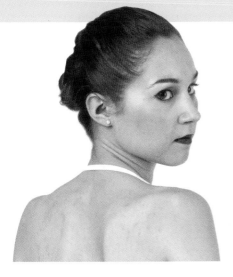

Curtain up

If a girl is otherwise well covered by her clothes, she may sit on a chair with her skirt well down towards ankles or knees, then let it 'ride up' in tiny increments to expose a few extra centimetres of flesh over a period of minutes. It's done so artfully that the male onlooker is only peripherally aware of what is happening – but he won't find it disagreeable.

Looking over a shoulder

Female shoulders are full of erotic significance to men – some finding them more interesting even than breasts or buttocks. This gesture, performed best wearing a strapless evening dress, gives the male a brief eyeful of shoulder combined with a sideways 'peeping Tom' glance for extra effect.

'serious-but-appealing' look (right). Could there be a hint of a smile in her eyes? Perhaps she knows that if there definitely was, he'd take it as encouragement. Better, for now, to keep him guessing.

Women attracting men

Legs twined

Often used deliberately, this pose emphasizes the sleek shape of the female legs very effectively. When a woman is wearing a skirt it tends to expose an extra length of thigh.

Legs crossed so a knee points

Often seen when a woman is sitting on a sofa with a man that she's interested in next to her. The knee points directly at him. Sometimes a girl will cross her legs and slip one foot partially free from the shoe; at others, the foot moves slowly in and out of the shoe, with an obvious innuendo.

Mouth and lips

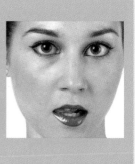

Mouth slightly open and lips moistened, whether by make-up or saliva, are said to be a sign of sexual invitation – lipstick is thought to have been used since earliest times to enhance the attractiveness of the lips. In practice, of course, most women wear some make-up, and have their mouths open some of the time, so these signs are not a very reliable guide.

Crossing and uncrossing the legs

Perhaps this is a variation on the sideways glance (see page 130). The legs are crossed, uncrossed, then re-crossed the other way several times during a conversation. It can be done so naturally and innocently that the male onlooker hardly realizes he is being invited to take in the agreeable female leg shape, emphasized by crossing and uncrossing. But it may give him the feeling that 'things are going OK'.

Good sign

If a man finds a female standing or walking close to his side, she probably finds him attractive.

Bad sign

If you notice her handbag is somehow always between you and her, it could mean she doesn't want you to touch her. Women use portable objects – typically handbags, but also umbrellas and briefcases – as barriers; or they may keep their hands in their pockets.

Hand gestures as greetings originated in earliest prehistory – perhaps to show that you carried no weapon and therefore meant no harm. Millennia later, the standard European or North American handshake is the internationally understood business greeting. However, few would want to argue with the necessity of knowing other prominent forms of greeting.

The main ones are the *salaam*, used by Muslims (and described on pages 142–3); the *namaste*, a Hindu greeting (described on page 150); and the Oriental bow (see page 155).

Besides describing essentials of meeting and greeting, this section will acquaint you with many other important details of behaviour you could encounter when travelling on business.

It also offers clues about behaviour that you should avoid as likely to cause offence wherever in the world you travel.

International etiquette

International etiquette

Europe

Because Europe has such a wide range of cultures, acceptable behaviour varies greatly between countries. Southern Europeans generally are thought to be more open and expressive than their more northern counterparts.

Finland

▶ Men and women, and often children, will shake hands when introduced.

▶ Open displays of emotion are unusual.

▶ Making and keeping direct eye contact is important in conversation.

▶ Standing with your arms folded will be interpreted as arrogance.

▶ If you want to cross your legs, do so at the knees not your ankles.

▶ Finns do not eat food on the street, except perhaps ice cream.

▶ Never eat with your fingers, not even fruit.

▶ It is considered bad manners to leave food on a

Finland: Don't fold your arms while standing as it will be be seen as arrogant.

plate, so only take small portions that you know you will be able to finish.

Britain

▶ The British are reputed to be slightly colder than their neighbours in mainland Europe and the handshake is the main formal greeting. It is not used on informal occasions, and younger people use it less than older ones.

▶ Hugs and kisses are very rare outside the family and circles of friends.

▶ Politeness and deference are important. Most British people wait patiently in queues; anyone trying to push in out of turn can bring protests.

▶ There's increasing restraint in some businesses over drinking alcohol at business lunches.

Czech Republic and Slovakia

▶ You may find, especially at formal meetings, that everyone shakes hands when they arrive and leave. Otherwise, Czechs and Slovaks do not indulge in physical contact in public.

▶ When eating, don't put your elbows on the table.

When you have finished your meal, put your knife and fork together parallel at one side of the plate. Leaving your knife and fork criss-crossed on the plate will be taken to mmean that you are just pausing.

Formal toasting is quite common at business meals. The host will take the lead and you should respond when you are invited.

Denmark

Handshakes are mostly firm and short.

If you are greeting a couple, shake hands with the woman first.

Children are taught to offer a handshake and maintain eye contact.

Politeness is important. Women go first through doors and down stairs; men go first up stairs.

Turning your back on people is impolite: for example, if you need to pass people in order to reach your seat, face them and say thank you.

You should bring clothes specifically for formal dinners.

At formal dinners each man will be presented with a card with the name of the female dining partner who will be sitting on his right. He should escort her to the table.

When eating, don't put your elbows on the table.

Toasting is popular. The correct form is to look around the group or toast one person, take a small sip and then make eye contact again.

France

Handshakes are quick, single, frequent up-and-down pumps.

In general, a man should wait for a woman to offer her hand first.

Czech Republic: It is usual to shake hands with everyone when they arrive or leave.

International etiquette

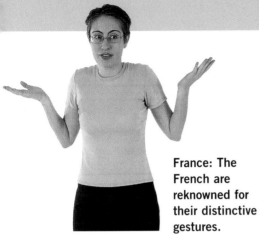

France: The French are reknowned for their distinctive gestures.

▶ Even with people they know well the French don't kiss on the cheek – they just touch cheeks and kiss air.

▶ They don't smile at strangers.

▶ Business cards are often exchanged. If you give a card to a superior, you may not necessarily get one in return.

▶ At business meetings, don't remove your jacket before the most senior person.

▶ Although the French gesture often, in work situations body language and behaviour tend to be restrained. Distinctive examples include pointing to the eye ('You can't fool me.') and a shrug, with the palms extended ('It doesn't bother me.') or with the palms raised chest-high ('What do you expect me to do about it?').

▶ To call a waiter, wait to catch his or her eye, raise your hand and say, 'Monsieur', 'Madame' or 'S'il vous plaît'.

Germany

▶ Men give a firm handshake perhaps with just one pump.

▶ Women and children will also shake hands, but less forcefully than men.

▶ When meeting a group, shake hands with each person.

▶ Do not keep your other hand in your pocket when shaking hands – it is seen as conveying disrespect.

▶ Business cards are exchanged as a matter of routine.

▶ In restaurants, the *maître d'* might seat strangers with you if there's a lack of space. This is common and you are not obliged to talk to them.

▶ Germans don't routinely say 'Please' and 'Thank you'. This isn't rude.

▶ Whether in a restaurant or at someone's home, don't cut potatoes, pancakes or dumplings with a knife: this implies that they are tough.

France: When greeting each other, the French touch cheeks and kiss air.

Hungary

▶ Shaking hands is the norm when anyone arrives or leaves.

▶ Men should wait for a woman to offer her hand.

▶ Hungarians are relatively non-tactile and like to maintain personal space: people stand about an arm's length apart.

▶ Wait to be introduced at formal parties.

Greece

▶ When greeting people, Greeks give a warm, friendly handshake, making plenty of eye contact, perhaps accompanied by a kiss on each cheek.

▶ 'No' is indicated by a slight upward nod, or raising the eyebrows, while tilting the head to either side in an up-and-down motion means 'Yes'.

▶ It may be a bit confusing, but Greeks often smile when angry.

▶ Greeks don't queue.

Ireland

▶ Greet people with a firm handshake.

▶ Business cards are not exchanged as a matter of course.

▶ As in Britain, queues are orderly. Don't try to barge to the front.

The Netherlands

▶ Men, women and children all shake hands. Making direct eye contact is important.

▶ Unique Dutch gestures include tapping the elbow, to indicate unreliability, and grabbing an imaginary fly in front of you, to show that they think someone is crazy.

▶ At dinner, the hostess may serve herself first. Eat only when she does.

▶ Take small portions, as you should eat everything on your plate.

▶ Don't get up during meals.

Italy

▶ Italy is the most touch-friendly nation in Europe – acquaintances kiss cheeks and male friends will embrace or walk arm in arm.

▶ Even businessmen who have met a only couple of times will offer a lingering handshake, perhaps clasping the other man's elbow, but this is not an appropriate gesture between men and women.

▶ The best-known Italian gesture is the shoulder shrug with raised hands to indicate 'I don't know'.

▶ Flicking the chin with a finger indicates impatience.

International etiquette

Norway

▶ Handshakes in Norway are brief and firm.

▶ Away from friends and family, and especially in work situations, the Norwegians tend not to be tactile. Don't put your arm around someone, or slap anyone on the back.

▶ Toast by making eye contact, lifting the glass to eye-level, say '*Skoal*', drink and make eye contact again.

Poland

▶ It is customary to shake hands andshakes when you meet someone and when you leave.

▶ Older Polish men may kiss women's hands, but Poles in general are not especially tactile, except with their family and friends.

▶ A useful gesture to understand is the the finger-flick against the neck that means 'Join me in a vodka'.

Portugal

▶ As with other Latin countries, firm, warm handshakes are the norm.

▶ The Portuguese are not very demonstrative, except in meeting close

Norway: The 'Skoal' toast is a Norwegian ritual.

friends, when men might slap each other's backs and women might embrace.

▶ They use only a few hand gestures. Flicking your chin with a finger means that you don't know the answer, while flicking it with a thumb means that something no longer exists.

Russia and the former Soviet Union

▶ Direct eye contact and a good firm handshake may be followed, for male friends, by a Russian bear hug, perhaps with quick kisses to alternate cheeks.

▶ Whistling at something or someone indicates disapproval.

▶ Passing in front of people with your back to them, for instance at the theatre or in a crowd, is taboo.

▶ When you enter a Russian home, don't shake hands over the threshold. Wait until you are inside.

▶ Russians don't smile at strangers, especially not in public. In private, however, you may see uninhibited displays of emotion, compared with, say, Britain or the USA.

Spain

▶ Handshakes are warm and friendly, and perhaps a man will pat someone he knows on the back or shoulder. The *abrazo* (embrace) is common, as it is in all Latin countries. Eye contact is important, although women need to be careful that it doesn't get confused with signalling interest.

▶ Spanish people value old-fashioned, formal behaviour – many hold strong conservative and religious values.

Russia: Male friends in Russia will often hug enthusiatically when they meet.

Spain: Offer a warm handshake and shoulder clasp.

▶ Keeping your hands in your pockets during a conversation will be considered rud by members of th older generation.

▶ The Spanish do not appreciate yawning or stretching in public.

▶ When arriving at a table in a restaurant or at someone's home, men usually make a point of waiting for all the women to sit down before they do so themselves.

▶ To toast, say 'chin chin' and clink glasses. Don't start to eat before everyone is seated, and always say '*Buen provecho*', ('Enjoy your meal.').

Switzerland

▶ Swiss customs naturally divide into French, German and Italian forms. Swiss-German greetings are short, firm and without any other touching, whereas the French and Italian versions involve embraces and cheek-kissing.

141

International etiquette

▶ Have plenty of business cards as they will get used.

▶ The Swiss especially appreciate an upright stance and good posture. Don't slouch in your chair or lean back with legs stretching out forwards.

▶ Swiss people find dropping litter particularly offensive (and the fines are very heavy).

▶ In a restaurant, strangers might take any seats that happen to be empty at your table.

Sweden

▶ Handshakes are firm and brief, with one or two pumps only. No other form of body contact takes place.

▶ Maintain eye contact when talking; it shows you're interested in what they're saying.

▶ Crossing your arms is not seen as defensive in Sweden but rather shows that you are listening.

▶ Swedes are serious, undemonstrative people and, perhaps more than most, tend to regard loud, extrovert behaviour as shallow.

▶ When talking to someone, keep your trunk face-on; angling yourself even slightly away from them could be taken as lack of interest.

▶ Swedes have a special dislike of being interrupted when talking; and of moving on to another subject before it is dealt with fully.

▶ Like other Scandinavians Swedes toast with the word '*Skoal*'.

Sweden: Watch your 'body axis'.

Middle East and the Arab world

There are a number of basic rules for etiquette in Arabic countries. These are listed here and specific advice for how to behave in each country is listed on the following pages.

▶ The standard greeting in Islamic and Arabic-speaking countries is the *salaam*. This is done by touching your heart with your right palm, then sweeping your forearm up and outward, with the words '*Essalam ëalaikum*,' ('Peace be with you.'). An abbreviated *salaam* is made by moving your forehead forward slightly and touching it with your fingertips.

▶ Arab men do a lot of touching. Handshaking is often prolonged, and men who know one another well may clasp elbows.

▶ The personal zone is smaller than in the West. Men will stand much closer to other men when holding a conversation than is usual in the West. To move away during a conversation is considered rude.

▶ This does not extend to women. Men and women stand farther apart than in the West, and there are no public displays of affection. Visiting men should wait for an Arabic woman to offer her hand.

▶ A man greeting another man who he does not know well will shake hands, whereas a man greeting a woman who he does not know well will touch his heart with his right palm.

▶ Avoid pointing, and never point directly at another person. This is the height of rudeness.

▶ Always remove your shoes before entering a house or a mosque.

▶ The sole of the shoe or foot is the lowest and dirtiest part of the body, and it is a profound insult to show it to or point it at someone.

▶ Use only the right hand for eating, and for presenting or receiving gifts. The left hand is used solely for hygiene purposes in any Islamic country.

▶ At meal times, Arabs will serve plenty of strong, thick, syrupy coffee in small cups. To indicate that you have had enough, tip the cup back and forth with your fingers.

Egypt

▶ Although Egyptians are used to Westerners, you should dress modestly. Men should wear long trousers. Women should wear long skirts or loose-fitting trousers, loose tops with high necklines and sleeves that cover the elbows.

▶ A lot of people in Egypt smoke and doing so in public is not frowned on.

Iran

▶ Handshakes are customary and shaking hands with children indicates respect for their parents.

▶ Women should wear a loose ankle-length skirt with a big, baggy, long-sleeved shirt or shirt and loose-fitting

International etiquette

mid-thigh-length jacket. Socks and a headscarf and also mandatory. Make-up and any jewellery apart from plain rings such as a wedding ring should be avoided in order not to cause offence and provoke strong reactions.

▶ Men must wear full-length trousers, and keep their arms covered.

Jordan

▶ Jordan is relatively westernized, but immodest dress may upset people. Women should wear at least knee-length dresses or trousers and cover their shoulders.

▶ In Jordan, politeness is an elaborate art. For example, at dinner if you are offered additional food, you should refuse twice, and only accept on the third time of offering. It is polite to leave small portions uneaten.

▶ Although Jordan is one of the few Arabic countries where alcohol is readily available, drinking anything more than modest amounts is frowned on.

Israel

▶ Hebrew is a very expressive language, and is accompanied by much touching and hand-holding between friends.

The *salaam* and the abbreviated version are standard greetings in the Arabic world.

▶ Visiting women should wait for an Israeli man to offer to shake hands. Women should avoid smiling at strangers, who might get the wrong impression.

▶ Orthodox Jews do not touch hands casually or shake hands between genders, even when passing business cards.

Palestine and the Occupied Territories

▶ When visiting Palestine, the Gaza Strip or the West Bank towns both men and women should keep their legs covered and women should also keep their shoulders and upper arms covered.

Men and women stand farther apart than in the West.

In Arabic countries handshakes are often enthusiastic and prolonged.

Saudi Arabia

▶ At political gatherings, you might see men greeting dignitaries and elders by kissing the right shoulder front to show their respect.

▶ Saudis may host joint business meetings in one room, with the host moving from one group to the next and back again.

▶ If your host interrupts a meeting and is gone for 20 minutes without explanation, it is for prayers.

▶ A nod means 'Yes', while tipping the head backwards and clicking the tongue means 'No'.

▶ Non-Westernized Saudis find crossing your legs disrespectful.

145

International etiquette

- ▶ Women, even Westerners, are not allowed to drive.
- ▶ Don't expect to be introduced to a veiled woman in the company of a Saudi man.
- ▶ Women should keep their legs, shoulders and arms covered at all times, in loose clothing.You may also need to cover your head with a scarf.
- ▶ Smoking in public is not common. In some places they will pass round a hookah (communal pipe).
- ▶ Alcohol and pork are illegal.
- ▶ Don't smoke, drink or eat in public during the holy month of Ramadan: you risk being sent to prison, possibly until the fast is over.

Turkey

- ▶ In addition to the normal handshakes, friends may put their hands over yours, or even embrace you.
- ▶ At an office or formal gathering, shake everyone's hand.
- ▶ A much younger person may kiss your hand and press it to his head as a sign of respect.
- ▶ Smoking and eating on the street are considered impolite

Turkey: If someone tips his head back and closes his eyes, it means 'No'.

- ▶ Show particular respect to elders, who are valued here.
- ▶ When talking, don't cross your arms or put your hands in your pockets.
- ▶ 'No' is indicated by raising the head a little, tipping it back and closing the eyes, or opening the eyes wide and raising the eyebrows.

Lebanon

- ▶ Children are taught not to talk unless addressed by a visitor.
- ▶ A nod means 'Yes', while a sharp upward motion of head and raised eyebrows means 'No'.
- ▶ In urban areas the Lebanese are quite tolerant of Western ways and dress, but in rural areas people are more traditional. Outside cities and the larger towns, Western women should take care to dress modestly.

Africa

▶ There is much ethnic diversity within each African country, but Western conventions will, by and large, be understood in capital cities and more developed areas. The handshake is the commonest greeting. There is little public contact between the sexes.

▶ Use the right hand for eating and giving and receiving things: in Muslim parts of Africa the left hand is used for hygiene purposes only.

▶ If you're offered a gift, accept it with grace; to refuse it would bring shame on the giver.

▶ Containers of water or homebrew beer may be passed around from person to person. However, it is not customary to share coffee, tea or bottled soft drinks.

Southern Africa

▶ Great emphasis is placed on handshakes. Try to pick up the local variations by watching what other people do. Western handshakes will be acceptable in most situations.

▶ Make time to learn the local words for 'Hello' and 'Goodbye': it will be appreciated.

▶ Before eating, diners may pass around a bowl of water for washing hands.

Congo

▶ Outside the capital, Kinshasa, many different tribal cultures make for diversity of manners. In the capital, the handshake is the usual form of greeting.

▶ Dining is an important social ritual: your manners may be watched closely. If the host uses his fingers for eating, follow this lead, but only use the right hand.

Ghana

▶ Western European and American etiquette is widely followed in work situations.

▶ Children are trained not to look at adults – it is seen as defiant.

Kenya

▶ Western European handshakes are common in business situations as are other 'Western' forms of etiquette, but outside the capital and other large centres there are many tribal cultures. Watch out for local variations.

International etiquette

Mali

▶ Northwest Mali follows Islamic customs. Take off your shoes before entering a home or a mosque, and be aware of other Muslim habits such as not pointing or showing the soles of your feet or shoes to anyone.

Morocco

▶ Most of Morocco is Islamic: see the general notes on correct forms of behaviour throughout the Arab World, pages 142–3.

▶ In Morocco handshakes are warm and hearty and closer aquaintances may fleetingly kiss the back of the each others fingers as a mark of particular respect.

Morocco: As in most Muslim countries, shoes are always taken off when going into someone's home or a mosque, as well as at meal times.

▶ Friends hug and place their cheeks together on either side twice, or four times for really close friends. However, this is completely innapropriate behaviour for strangers.

▶ Don't use your left hand to exchange money, or for any unnecessary contact.

▶ Modest dress is a must for both sexes so avoid any display of flesh and wear loose clothes.

▶ Public displays of affection between couples are frowned upon, even those who are married.

▶ Meals are eaten sitting cross-legged on the floor at low tables. You can eat with the fingers of your right hand.

▶ Morocco is a very hospitable country, and strangers are often invited into family homes, where guests may be invited to carry out a pre-dinner ablution ritual, where water from a kettle is poured over the hands into a basin.

Nigeria

▶ It is hard to generalize about greetings in Nigeria because local tribal cultures are so diverse. In the major centres, Western forms of greeting will rarely be taken amiss.

Sudan

▶ The country is Arab-influenced, especially the north. See the general observations on etiquette in the Arab world, pages 142–3.

Australasia

Australia and New Zealand

▶ Australians and New Zealanders greet with a firm friendly handshake.

▶ Making and maintaining proper eye contact is very important in business meetings.

▶ When asked, 'How're you doing/going?' the correct response to make is, 'I'm good/fine. How're you?', not to give a detailed description of your state of health.

▶ Business cards are exchanged, but it is not such an important ritual as it is in, for example, Japan or Germany.

▶ Australians and New Zealanders tend to appreciate open, informal manners and behaviour, but may not appprove of strongly-expressed emotions, which could well be seen as gushing.

▶ The Polynesian Maoris – the native New Zealanders – greet by pressing noses.

▶ Among Australian men, a slap on the back tends to be the limit of physical expressions of friendship and respect.

▶ Yawning without covering the mouth is more-than-usually frowned on by Australians, who will often add an 'Excuse me' as well.

▶ Australians, like the British, respect queues: when standing in line, they do so in an orderly way, and anyone who does not wait in their proper place will have this pointed out to them, perhaps forcefully.

Fiji

▶ In greeting, Fijians nod and say '*Bula*' ('Welcome'). But they will shake hands with foreign visitors. Eye contact is good and there will be much laughter.

▶ When speaking, maintain direct eye contact, but don't hold it for too long.

▶ Shoes are removed before entering someone's home.

▶ It is rude to stay standing once inside a house, to touch somebody's head, or to decline gifts or food.

International etiquette

The Indian Subcontinent

▶ The main form of greeting, and farewell, on the Indian subcontinent is the *namaste*, a Hindu greeting which consists of the hands being held chest-high in prayer position accompanied by a slight bow.

▶ As in the Middle East, the soles of the shoes and feet are regarded as the dirtiest parts of body. Shoes should always be removed when entering a temple or a mosque.

▶ Women should always cover their heads in a temple or mosque.

▶ Use only the right hand for eating, presenting or receiving gifts, passing an object to someone, or pointing. The last should be done not with one finger (this is considered very rude) but with your whole hand.

Myanmar (Burma)

▶ Shaking hands is not customary in Myanmar, although people in business might do it.

▶ In Buddhism, the lower half of the body is regarded as lowly, and the upper half holy. You should not touch the head of an image of Buddha.

India

▶ Men do not touch women formally or informally. A Western woman should not try to shake hands with an Indian man. Indian women will shake hands with foreign women, but not men.

▶ Indian businessmen may show their appreciation with enthusiastic backslapping – don't be alarmed.

▶ Take plenty of business cards – Indians exchange them routinely.

▶ Always ask permission before smoking or taking photos: the latter can be a sensitive issue in any many parts of the world, but this is especially the case in India.

Indian subcontinent: The *namaste* is the main form of greeting.

India: Nodding the head from side to side indicates sincerity.

▶ Do not touch paintings or statues in temples or mosques.

▶ Public displays of affection are not considered proper, even between married couples.

▶ The head is regarded as a sacred part of the body, so do not touch anyone's head; even a child's.

▶ A unique Indian gesture is to grasp the earlobe to indicate either remorse or honesty depending on the context.

▶ Nodding the head from side to side is another characteristically Indian gesture, indicating sincerity.

Pakistan

▶ The country is Islamic. Handshakes are customary when meeting people, and friends of the same sex might embrace. Men may sometimes be seen holding hands when walking.

▶ Greetings are often accompanied by an offer of coffee or tea which you should not refuse.

▶ Be careful about gender customs. A Western man should not shake hands with a Pakistani woman unless she offers her hand, although a Western woman may offer to shake hands with a Pakistani man.

▶ Don't photograph Pakistani women without permission.

▶ Greetings are often accompanied by an offer of coffee or tea which you should always accept.

Sri Lanka

▶ Handshaking is usual, as well as the *ayubowan*, a variation on the *namaste*. Women shake hands with Westerners of both sexes, but Western men shouldn't embrace women when greeting.

▶ People may smile instead of saying thank you, but you should be aware that a smile can also be seen as flirtatious.

▶ If someone is reluctant to sit down with you, don't insist, as there is a strong caste system. You will only embarrass them by doing so.

▶ Images of Buddha are sacred, so don't touch or lean on them.

International etiquette

China: It is usual for bowls to be held very close to the face.

China and the Far East

Bangladesh

▶ About 85 per cent of Bengalis are Muslims, so they will greet you with the *salaam*. About 12 per cent of the population is Hindu, and they will use the *namaste*.

▶ As elsewhere in the Islamic world, you should always be sensitive to gender divisions. Bengali men will shake hands with Western man, but will only nod at a woman.

▶ You should take off your shoes upon entering a mosque, and wash your feet if other people are doing so. You should also take your shoes off when entering someone's home.

▶ Don't take photographs of people in Bangladesh without obtaining clear permission beforehand.

▶ Men and women often dine separately.

▶ Don't visit the washroom during a meal, only before or after.

China

▶ The Western handshake is becoming the most common form of greeting, especially in business, but a nod or bow is fine.

▶ Guests are introduced to Chinese people in order of their hosts' seniority.

▶ Business cards will probably be exchanged next, and should, ideally, be in your language and in Chinese. Present cards with both hands as this is more respectful.

▶ Next, everyone sits and Chinese tea is served, usually in a lidded teacup with leaves floating on top. Blow the leaves lightly to the other side of the cup or use the lid to brush them off.

▶ The Chinese are generally non-tactile people, but they stand closer than Westerners. The young display affection publicly more than they used to.

▶ The Chinese like to applaud, even as a form of greeting; you should always applaud back.

▶ Chinese people do not like to say no, and may shake their heads in silence if they don't like what you're asking.

▶ In the cities there is not much eye contact in public, although you might get stared at in smaller places.

▶ Silence is a virtue, a sign of politeness and contemplation. During conversation, try not to interrupt.

▶ Food bowls are held under the chin. Wait for the host to pick up his chopsticks before eating. The Chinese may rub chopsticks to remove possible splinters, but it would be impolite for a visitor to do so, as it suggests your hosts would give you cheap chopsticks.

▶ Refusing food is also considered impolite.

▶ Chinese etiquette is to decline gifts two or three times before accepting them even if they are wanted.

Indonesia

▶ Indonesia consists of 17,000 islands and some 300 ethnic groups, so across the whole country gestures and behaviour vary greatly. But for urban areas a few general points can apply, particularly for business purposes.

▶ A handshake plus a slight nod is customary for greeting, congratulating or parting, for both sexes. Aside from this, men do not touch women in public. You should always use people's titles to address them.

▶ In West Java, they use a Thai greeting, with the palms together, fingertips towards chin and a nod.

▶ Indonesians do not like to show feelings, especially negative ones. They don't like to disappoint people, so they avoid disagreeing in public and smile to hide shock or embarrassment. You should avoid showing excessive gratitude or outbursts of anger.

Japan: In Japan, however, eating bowls are held relatively low.

International etiquette

▶ The sole of the shoe is a taboo, the right hand is used far more than the 'unclean' left; pointing with fingers is very rude and touching people's heads is not advisable.

▶ When dining, leave a little food. A clear plate means you want more.

Hong Kong

▶ The conventional handshake is the most common greeting. The Chinese people do not like body contact, though men may hold hands when walking. They may also stand fairly close by Western standards.

▶ Don't blink too much as here it can be interpreted as a sign of boredom or lack of interest.

▶ At mealtimes, Chinese and Western customs will sometimes be mixed. Chopsticks, for example, may be used in conjunction with knives and forks either for different dishes or different courses.

▶ Tea may be served during meetings. If the host leaves his tea untouched for a long time, this may be an indication that he considers the meeting to be over.

Japan and South Korea: Exchanging business cards is an important business ritual.

Japan

▶ Bowing is of course the traditional greeting in Japan. The Western handshake is also widespread, but with a lighter grip. Most Japanese find direct eye contact intimidating.

▶ Overt displays of emotion are unwelcome. The tiniest gestures have meaning, so be careful to limit your own hand and arm gestures.

▶ Business card etiquette is perhaps more important than anywhere else (see page 26).

▶ Listening attentively and not interrupting are crucial. Never raise your voice or be 'upfront'. The Japanese don't like to say no, so be aware that nodding does not necessarily signal agreement.

▶ White gauze masks are common if people have colds.

▶ Japanese chopstick etiquette is much like China's; the major difference is that food bowls are held lower. You should pick up dishes on your left side with your right hand and vice versa.

▶ A common Japanese toast is '*Kan-pai*' ('Drain the cup').

▶ Remove your shoes when entering a home or restaurant.

South Korea

▶ Bowing is the traditional form of greeting, perhaps combined with a handshake if greeting Westerners. Women don't shake hands, just nod.

▶ Deference to rank and elders is important. The senior offers to shake hands first; the junior bows first.

▶ Koreans are taught to avoid eye contact, and a youngster making eye contact with an elder is regarded as displaying defiance.

▶ As in Japan, read business cards thoroughly and keep them to hand.

▶ Walking directly behind people can be considered impolite so try to avoid it.

▶ Koreans avoid saying 'no' by tipping their heads back and sucking air.

▶ Laughter is used to cover-up all sorts of emotions.

▶ It is disrespectful to pour your own drink – the host should do it – or to open gifts at the time they are given.

Malaysia

▶ The Malaysian population is made up of 5 per cent Malays (Muslim), 32 per cent Chinese and 11 per cent Indians. The handshake is used

International etiquette

universally. Within the Chinese population, men and women will shake hands with each other, but not with Indians or Malays.

▶ Malays greet with the *salaam*, but theirs differs slightly from the Arab version: they simply extend the hands, putting the fingertips together, then place the hands on the chest. Indians greet with the *namaste*.

▶ Other traits divide the population along religious and cultural lines. For Malays and Indians, the head is sacred and should not be touched.

▶ Before entering Malay mosques and homes, you should remove your shoes and leave them with everyone else's.

▶ Don't stand on prayer mats or touch them with your feet.

▶ In this part of the world Indians shake their heads to indicate agreement.

Philippines

▶ There has long been an American presence in the Philippine Islands, so Western gestures are familiar. Handshakes are the norm for men, women and children. Quickly raising the eyebrows is another informal greeting.

▶ In public, two women may hold hands, but men do not.

▶ Filipino taboos include staring, talking loudly, and women smoking in public.

▶ Laughter serves to hide other emotions such as anger or embarrassment.

▶ At meals, always leave some food on your plate to indicate that the host has served enough. An empty plate indicates that you would like more.

▶ Filipinos will point to something not with the hands, which is seen as rude, but with their eyes, or even sometimes with pursed lips.

Thailand

▶ The Thai greeting is called the *wai*: the hands are held together as if in prayer, and the head nodded in a slight bow, very like the Indian *namaste*. The *wai* can be used for greeting, parting, gratitude and apology. The higher the hands, the more respectful the greeting, but the fingertips should not be higher than the face.

▶ Remove your shoes when entering someone's home, even though some Thais defer to the West and will let you keep them on.

▶ Don't step on the doorsill as Thais

believe that a deity lives there.

▶ The head is sacred, so don't touch it, while the feet are lowly, so don't point them or show the soles.

▶ Patting someone's back or shoulders is offensive.

▶ Two men might hold hands when walking, but otherwise there are no public displays of affection.

▶ Thais particularly dislike loud, boisterous or aggressive behaviour; don't talk in a raised voice, and never show anger during negotiations.

Thailand: The *wai* **greeting is very like the Indian** *namaste.*

▶ Latin Americans generally like touching and expressions of warmth. They greet with warm handshakes perhaps with both hands. For friends, there is the *abrazo* (embrace). Women may kiss each other on the cheek.

▶ Eye contact is very important. They will stand much closer than Europeans or North Americans.

▶ Generally used gestures across the continent include tugging the corner of the eye downward with one finger to indicate 'Be careful,' tapping the elbow for 'cheap' and flicking the back of the fingers under the chin to mean 'I don't know'.

Tahiti

▶ Carefully shake hands with everyone present. You may find people kissing each other on the cheeks, as in France – a relic of French occupation.

Singapore

▶ The population includes Chinese, Muslims and Indians.

▶ Manners may show British influences, since Singapore was once part of the British Empire. The handshake is the

157

standard greeting, perhaps combined with a slight bow for Asians.

▶ Women make the first move when shaking hands.

▶ Don't touch anyone on the top of the head and don't touch or move anything with your feet.

▶ The old are held in great respect: people usually rise when they enter a room and give up seats for them in public places.

▶ Singapore is a very clean and tidy country and there are severe local penalties – typically large fines – for dropping litter, even cigarette ends.

Samoa

▶ Greetings are formal and somewhat flowery speeches. Eloquence is a Samoan speciality.

▶ When visiting a home, wait until a mat has been laid down before entering, then remove your shoes. Sit cross-legged on the mat. Conversation tends to take place only when people are seated. Be careful not to point your feet at anyone.

▶ The Samoan national drink is called *kava*. It is traditional to spill a few drops before drinking.

Taiwan

▶ The handshake is the usual greeting, though a nod (with eyes cast downwards) is acceptable.

▶ Like other Asian countries, the Taiwanese respect business cards, which should be read carefully and kept to hand.

▶ The elderly are treated with great deference.

▶ Here, 'No' is indicated by holding the hand up at facelevel, with the palm out and moveing it back and forth.

▶ Toast by saying '*kan-pei*'.

▶ Use both hands to give and receive presents.

Brazil: This gesture means 'What do you expect?' in Brazil.

Central and South America

Bolivia

▶ Women are expected to dress modestly. Trousers should be loose and skirts should fall on or below the knee.

▶ Time and time-keeping are not seen as important in Boliva.

▶ Nothing in Bolivia is eaten with the fingers, not even fruit, which is eaten with a special fork.

Argentina

▶ Women will probably not talk to strangers unless introduced.

▶ Argentinians are demonstrative, and greet each other by kissing on the cheek.

▶ Gestures are important. Brushing the tips of the fingers of one hand outward, under the jaw and chin, with the palm of the hand toward the neck, means 'I don't know, I don't care, who knows?' Bunching the fingertips of one hand together, pointing them slightly upwards, then moving your hand up and down a few times means 'What do you expect?'

▶ The correct toast is 'salud' ('health').

▶ Drinking mate (pronounced 'mah-tay'), or Paraguayan tea, is an important ritual. Never refuse if offered.

Brazil

▶ In Portuguese-speaking Brazil, the embrace is called the abraáo, and the toast is 'saude'

▶ Business cards are always exchanged at meetings.

▶ A Brazilian might pinch his earlobe to express appreciation. The fig gesture – fist thumb-up between index and middle finger – means good luck in Brazil (elsewhere it is rude), while punching the cupped hand with a fist is vulgar. Snapping the fingers while whipping the hand out and down is done for emphasis.

▶ Time-keeping is not important. It is normal for Brazilians to arrive an hour or so late for appointments.

Costa Rica

▶ Greetings are very important. Men shake hands when meeting and departing, while women kiss each other on the cheek, although in business circumstances they may shake hands.

International etiquette

Business is conducted in a very formal manner, with jackets kept on and no *abrazos* (embraces). Business cards are exchanged routinely on meeting, and, ideally, should be in both English and Spanish.

Appearances and first impressions are very important here: dress conservatively and be agreeable and friendly.

United States of America: The wink conveys many different meanings.

Chile

Holding up the palm and spreading the fingers out means 'stupid'.

Never eat with fingers.

Guatemala, Belize and Yucatan

Greetings here are hearty and involve a lot of eye contact. To gesture goodbye, raise your hand, with the palm facing you and wave the fingers back and forth.

Politeness is very important in Latin America. When talking to someone in Spanish-speaking parts of the region start your conversation with '*Buenos dias*' or '*Buenas tardes*' and a smile.

When you enter a room, it's polite to say '*Buenos dias*' as a general greeting to everyone in the room.

When leaving a restaurant, wish the other diners '*Buen provecho*'.

Honduras

Waving the index finger back and forth on a level with the chin is the Honduran gesture for 'No'.

Bargaining is expected when shopping.

Mexico

Mexicans are very touch-friendly. Men let women make the first move when handshaking. An embrace (*abrazo*) and some back-patting may be introduced at subsequent meetings. In some areas, after handshaking, they slide the hands upwards to grasp each other's thumbs. The handshake even may be drawn out by touching the forearms or fondling the other man's lapels.

▶ Bargaining is expected in markets and small shops, but not in big stores.

▶ Traditional family ties are very strong, and an invitation into a family home is a great honour.

▶ Women in particular should dress modestly, and everyone should dress respectfully to go into a church.

North America

Canada

▶ Firm handshakes with direct eye contact are standard. Canadians tend to be comparatively reserved, and do not do much gesturing. They are generally not especially tactile, except, perhaps, for some embarrassed back-slapping.

▶ Quebec, the French-speaking province, follows many French customs.

United States of America

▶ Firm handshakes with confident eye contact are the norm. Men tend to see hugging as an affront to masculinity, and even women do not hug and kiss as much as they do in Europe, except in communities that have imported their home country's customs.

▶ The advancement of sexual equality in the workplace and other areas of life means that the deference to women in the form of chivalry, still innocently demonstrated in Europe, could be regarded as politically incorrect in the US.

▶ Silent gaps in conversation may make Americans especially uncomfortable.

▶ Whistling does not denote derision, as it does in Europe. By contrast, it accompanies applause.

▶ Visitors may notice that winking is comparatively common. This has various meanings, including friendliness, flirtation, or 'I'm kidding'.

▶ Always be punctual for any business or social occasion and dress appropriately. Lateness and sloppiness are seen as marks of a lack of respect.

▶ If someone asks, 'How are you?', respond with 'Very well', or 'Fine, thanks'.

▶ Don't smoke anywhere unless smoking is clearly permitted. In many states it is illegal to smoke anywhere in public and you will be fined at the least.

Positive body language

Smile with your eyes
see page 33

A trustworthy hand shake
see page 39

Appropriate body and foot pointing *see page 120*

Modulate your voice
and use open palms to indicate honesty. *see page 57*

Positive body language everyone should know

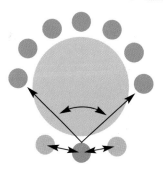

The business gaze
see page 90

Use the lighthouse technique when addressing groups or audiences
see page 59

Positive posture when seated
see page 125

Keep to the business zone when appropriate
see page 18

'I know this place' rather than **'I own this place'**
see page 99

Negative body language

Body angled away from an audience
see page 56

Strutting
and other over-dominant gestures
see page 95

Hand-to-face gestures
see page 108

Holding the gaze too long
when lying
see page 110

The downwards gaze
see page 89

**Bone crushing
handshakes**
see page 89

**Leaning back
and tilting
your head
back**
see page 29

**Steepling your
hands**
see page 88

Index

Index